ESCAPE THE TRAP OF COMPULSIVE EATING...

"Close your eyes and get comfortable...remember back to the most recent time you ate more than you wanted or started to eat even though you weren't hungry. Replay the incident slowly, frame by frame...does the scene feel familiar? Is this a time you usually overeat? Is this one of those persistently difficult times you have around food? Now, focus in on your emotional state just before you ate. How were you feeling...?"

With exercises such as this, **FAT IS A FEMINIST ISSUE II** gives you a step-by-step program to conquer compulsive eating. Author Susie Orbach has successfully worked with hundreds of women in overcoming their eating problems. A psychotherapist specializing in the treatment of compulsive eating, she is a co-founder of The Women's Therapy Centre of London and The Women's Therapy Center Institute of New York.

Also by Susie Orbach

FAT IS A FEMINIST ISSUE
FAT IS A FEMINIST ISSUE II
UNDERSTANDING WOMEN:
A FEMINIST PSYCHOANALYTIC APPROACH
(with Luise Eichenbaum)
WHAT DO WOMEN WANT
(with Luise Eichenbaum)

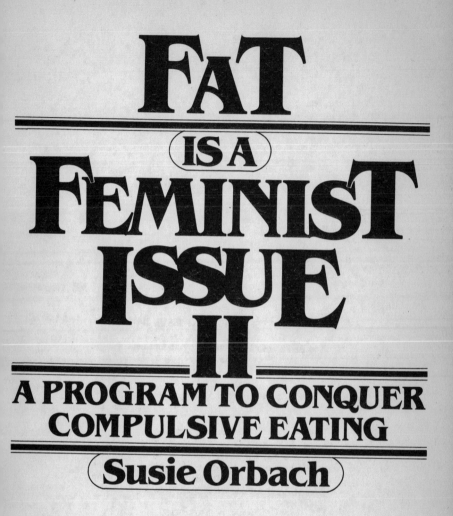

FAT
IS A
FEMINIST ISSUE II
A PROGRAM TO CONQUER COMPULSIVE EATING

Susie Orbach

BERKLEY BOOKS, NEW YORK

FAT IS A FEMINIST ISSUE II

A Berkley Book / published by arrangement with
the author

PRINTING HISTORY
Berkley trade paperback edition / September 1982

ISBN: 0-425-09387-5

10   9

ACKNOWLEDGEMENTS

Thanks to Nina Shandloff and Linda Healey for thoughtful editing, to Sara and Ed Lebar for housing me, to Judy Lever for discussion on compulsive eating and pregnancy, to all the women who replied to the questionnaire, to Mira Dana and The Women's Therapy Centre and to Sara Baerwald, Sally Berry, Carol Bloom, Luise Eichenbaum, Joseph Schwartz and Gillian Slovo for being who they are.

*To Clair Chapman
and the Spare Tyre Theatre Company*

CONTENTS

9

INTRODUCTION

Since *Fat Is A Feminist Issue* was published in the spring of 1978, I have received hundreds of letters from individual women about their eating problems. Many of these letters made it clear to me that women needed more detailed guidelines on how to translate the ideas in *Fat Is A Feminist Issue* into practice. Mira Dana, a student at the Women's Therapy Centre in London, and I prepared a questionnaire designed to identify the specific difficulties individual women were experiencing and the obstacles that self-help groups might be encountering in attempting to apply the theories in *Fat Is A Feminist Issue*. The questionnaire was sent out to women who had attended introductory workshops that used the *Fat Is A Feminist Issue* method. This method looks at the meaning of food in a woman's life and the unconscious associations to body images of fat and thin. It offers a way out of the compulsive eating syndrome by showing how to distinguish between physiological hunger and emotional hunger, and how to respond to each appropriately. After analyzing those answers and reflecting on the questions brought up most frequently by the group leaders I was training in this method, I decided it would be helpful to prepare *Fat Is A Feminist Issue II*, which is intended to be a very down-to-earth and practical guide to address the persistent bumps and barriers that many women experience in grappling with their eating problems.

Today several million people in America are on a diet or a weight-reduction scheme of one kind or another. Sadly we know that those methods work for very few people in the long run. Ninety-seven percent will regain the weight they worked so hard to lose, and the ones who didn't need to reduce their size in the first place will live in the grip of anxiety around food and will be constantly watching themselves. This book offers a different way to address the diet dilemma. It asks why we are fat and why we want to be thin, and it offers us a way to live more harmoniously in our bodies.

How to Use this Book

The main text and the psychological exercises in Part II of this book are meant to be used together. In Part I you will occasionally come across the symbol ❊ which denotes the introduction of a psychological exercise. I suggest you read through the entire book once to get a sense of how it is organized and where the exercises fit in, and then work through section by section as each feels appropriate for you. The exercises will help you get in touch with emotional states you may not be aware of, that are connected to your feelings about your body and your eating.

Keeping a Journal

In all your work with compulsive eating—be it fantasizing, answering the questions in the book, or in your day-to-day observations—you may find it useful to keep a diary or a notebook in which you jot down your reactions. Any insights you get can be written down immediately before you have time to "forget" or unconsciously reject them. Those women working on their food problem on their own will find it particularly useful to keep such a diary and use it when they set out to do their daily or weekly sessions. In this way you will have a record of your development that you can refer to from time to time.

You will notice that some of the material in the later part of the book is especially directed at groups. Most of this, however, is equally relevant to individual women working on the problem of compulsive eating alone or in pairs. Some of the practical issues of group work will be less relevant to individuals, but the information given should be helpful in demonstrating how well a group might work for you.

Though *Fat Is A Feminist Issue II* stands on its own, I have not attempted to recapitulate in detail all the concepts I explored in *Fat Is A Feminist Issue*. You may want to turn to *Fat Is A Feminist Issue* for further discussion of particular theoretical areas. *Fat Is A Feminist Issue II* will spell out in more detail the kinds of practical interventions that can be helpful in working on a compulsive-eating problem.

Susie Orbach
NEW YORK, 1981

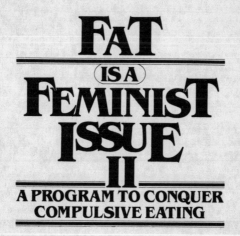

FAT IS A FEMINIST ISSUE II

A PROGRAM TO CONQUER COMPULSIVE EATING

PART I

CHAPTER I

The Roots
of the Problem

Habitual compulsive eating can become a painful and an engrossing problem, almost a way of life. People can get caught up in a syndrome in which they spend hours silently worrying and obsessing about what they should or should not be eating and, when they do allow themselves to eat, they end up not being able to really taste the food or gain much pleasure from it. Food and eating as a satisfying and unambivalent pleasure eludes the compulsive eater. Instead, food is used as a tool to help one cope—in the short term—with difficult feelings and emotional distress. Food then may become a narcotic, quelling the anxiety that unconfronted and unrecognized feelings raise. Compulsive eaters are out of touch with physiological cues that signal hunger or satisfaction. They look to food to meet all sorts of needs that may arise out of unconscious needs and conflicts. The activity of the eating and the preoccupation with food mask underlying problems.

Most treatment offered to those considered over- or underweight by doctors and dieticians focuses on manipulation of diet. In that treatment the strategy is to educate the patient, to get her or him (it's usually her) to understand the rules of the body. The main point made is that you can't take in more than your body needs without gaining weight. If this educational approach doesn't work, and the patient doesn't follow instructions, she is scolded. And if this doesn't work a whole range of artificial "fixes," from appetite depressants to stapling the jaws together, are available. But because compulsive eaters are psychologically addicted to food and patterns of bingeing and deprivation, such strategies rarely enable them to fundamentally change their eating patterns. Many people lose weight intermittently—some with ease, some with great difficulty—but they usually have a tremendously hard time maintaining that loss. The odds are that in a desperate search for a solution they will enroll at a diet clinic or return to the family doctor, or consult a specialist physician, or buy the latest best seller, and try to slim down again. *Their food problem hasn't been tackled.*

While the schemes offered by many diet books, doctors, and weight-loss organizations seem on the surface quite sensible—a matter of getting the right fuel for a particular engine—few people can view food in that simple utilitarian way. The meaning of food for each individual must be looked at. The food we eat, how we eat and how we feel about food are a reflection of who we are. How and what we eat derives substantially from what we first learned in our families, how we felt around the family table and in the kitchen with Grandma, and so on. The family meal in itself was an expression of the social meaning of food. Mealtimes are rituals of family and friends getting together. Food is imbued with layers and layers of meaning.

Women as Nurturers

Food has special meanings in the lives of women. Traditionally women are intimately involved in choosing, buying and cooking food. They are responsible for making sure that the family's food needs are adequately met. They are expected to cope with providing breakfast, school lunches, supper and any specialized food requirements. They manipulate the family budget skillfully so that if economic circumstances worsen, as they have for many families recently, they will not suffer nutritionally or feel the lack of previously available favorite foods. In other words, women are at the center of the household feeding pattern. On them rests basic responsibilities for the family's health and well-being. Because women of this generation were brought up to take on these responsibilities, such concerns may fall largely in their province even if they are in a non-traditional relationship or marriage. In fact, in a woman's psychology, an important aspect of her self-esteem derives from her ability to be a good nurturer—in perhaps a parallel sense the aspect of self-esteem that a man derives from his job and his capacity to be the economic provider.

If we take a look at almost any magazine that is directed at women, whether aimed at the working-class woman, the housewife—low or middle income—or the professional and business woman, the magazine will be full of advertisements from food manufacturers accompanied by copy on how to serve the most economic, time-saving, natural, healthy, sexy or elegant meals. A woman is assaulted page after page with reminders about her responsibility to feed others. The assumption is that women are the right people, in an almost biologically divined sense, to be concerned about food delivery. (Just check your own re-actions to a man who is a good cook. Don't you think he has something rather special.) At the same time, the not-so-subtle message of women's magazines and daytime television advertisements is that women cannot afford to rely on their judgment about what food is appropriate. They are deemed to need the constant guidance of "experts." Women are taught that, in this crucial area of their lives, they are always in danger of making mistakes. Libby's or Nestle knows best. At minimum the message is, there is always room for improvement in being a better provider.

Beyond getting the nutritional requirements right, the woman is en-couraged to express her unique personality through the food she pre-pares. Food becomes a medium through which she communicates many feelings. It demonstrates her love, her caring and her concern for her family. A woman's value rises with her ability to produce prettier, more economic, more wholesome and at the same time delectable meals, snacks and picnics.

The woman's traditional role of service in the food arena is both a real and a symbolic reflection of women's relation to society and the family. The sexes are still legally, economically and sexually unequal. Women are still directed into one sphere of human activity and men into another, more highly valued sphere. This means that, when all is said and done, the home, the family, having babies and bringing them up, and looking after the husband's needs, washing, cleaning, feeding, nurturing and so on are *felt* as constituting the true realm for women's activity and satisfaction. The contemporary woman who has grown up with all these pressures and is now attempting to express herself more broadly through her work, her job, her career, is often subject to a complex of ambivalent feelings about herself and her body too. She may feel ill at ease if she "sacrifices" a family for a career. She may find herself making a choice that is painful and limiting in another direction. She may feel resentful if she tries to juggle both roles, as those close to her often do not recognize the enormous demands she is trying to meet. Whichever way a woman tries to work out this dilemma, her struggle is set against an internal emotional background that nags at her, reminding her that, in order to be a "proper" woman, she must have a man to share her life with. And, in order to "catch and keep" a man, she must be attractive and appealing.

We Are Alienated From Our Bodies

A woman's body, then, becomes for her an instrument, a commodity that she can and must use in our world in the pursuit of her personal attempt to find contentment and a place. And, a woman's body, we learn, is not a very good or safe environment to live inside. Rarely are our mothers and other female adults able to convey to a young woman that her body, whatever natural shape it has, is a source of pride and of beauty, since they themselves have not been able to feel that. We learn instead that our bodies are powerful in a negative sense, they can destabilize men and get us into trouble. It is no wonder then that we become frightened of our bodies and see them not as where we live but as a part of us that we must control, watch and direct.

Because of this we automatically see ourselves with a critical eye. A woman's body can always use improving; our legs, our hair, our bustline, our skin, our cellulite are all in danger of being unseemly unless attended to in a feminine way. Encouraged to see ourselves this way, it is not surprising that we grow up alienated and scared of our bodies. A woman's body is one of the few culturally accepted ways a woman has to express herself and yet the scope of this expression is limited by a contradiction: the pressure to look a certain way, to conform to today's slim image.

Food Is For Others

A situation exists therefore where a woman's focuses on food and body image converge in a particularly intense way. In order to be feminine, she must present an attractive picture of herself, which today means a slender profile. Under this circumstance I think we can see just how significant food becomes in her life. Food is what she gives to *others* but must deprive herself of. Food is, if you like, good for *others* but somehow dangerous to the woman herself. Food is about health for *others*, but about beauty for herself. Food, it is alleged, does terrible things to women and one must be very careful approaching it. It can make you fat, spotty, ugly. It exposes your desires and your greed. Food, which is imbued with the spirit of giving when prepared for others, takes on a sinister face when women eat. A woman is meant to police her eating, to feel cautious of what she eats, to be constantly watching it. At the same time food is her way of caring for *others*. Food is her power in the family, it is a means by which she exerts incredible influence; she brings comfort, reward, reassurance through it.

For women food carries such complex meanings that it is nonsense to focus on calories or carbohydrate grams when working towards a plan to lose weight. The roots of compulsive eating in women stem from women's position in society—she feeds everyone else, but her needs are personally illegitimate. Food, therefore, can become a way to try to give to herself. Her fatness can become a way to express a protest at the definitions of her social role. Fatness, as an unspoken communication, can imply bigness, strength, motherliness, solidity; it can embrace any problem. Slimness equals beauty and attractiveness, and is elusive. For many women, fatness feels like a rejection of the packaged sexuality around us. We need to decipher the meaning of fatness to the individual, what it symbolizes, to understand why a woman has expressed herself through food and body image. To focus on calories is unrealistic in such circumstances. The focus must be shifted to the *meaning* of food in people's lives so that distortions of very basic psychological cues can be understood and then corrected. When we think about the meaning of food in our lives for just a few minutes, we advance from calories and perhaps tap feelings of pleasure, connectedness, fear, love, and so on. It is coming to grips with these kinds of themes in relation to food and body image that can enable the compulsive eater to relate to food in a positive way.

A Note About Anorexia

Much of what I have written here and in FIFI applies only in a very particular way to those women whose compulsive eating problems express themselves through anorectic symptoms. Some of the most obvious differences lie around the issue of control and responsibility in relation to food. Any woman who has suffered with anorexia will clearly feel that her eating problems aren't quite accurately described. Her experience is of the need to be totally in control. The food is so terrifying that she will have developed schemes, perhaps hourly strategies, to control her desire to eat. She is persistently and painfully involved with thoughts about food and what it might do to her. Her needs in a group will be quite different than those of women whose compulsive eating problems predominately show up in patterns of bingeing, dieting and "overweight" as opposed to bingeing, vomitting, starving and being painfully underweight. For this reason I am now inclined to suggest that women who suffer from the anorectic side of the syndrome would do best organized in groups specifically designed for them. Just as a compulsive eater can find that a group provides the first place for honest sharing, so too the anorectic woman can find safety and comfort in revealing herself with others who have similar experience. Anorexia involves hiding who you are, both from yourself and from others. In the process you may also become stealthy about what you do to protect yourself. In a group with other women who've taken the same route, there is the possibility of disclosing all the pain without fear of judgment, or shocked reactions, and this is tremendously important.

CHAPTER 2

Slimness: The New God?

Women come in all shapes and sizes. Some of us are short, some of us are tall. We can have short legs, medium-length legs, long legs, big breasts, medium-size breasts, small breasts, standing up breasts, floppy breasts, large, medium or small hips; we can be pear-shaped, broad or rounded, have flat stomachs, full stomachs, even teeth, crooked teeth, large eyes, dimpled cheeks. But the extraordinary variety that is woman's body is systematically ignored in our culture. The richness of our different shapes is reduced to the overriding image of slimness. Advertisements for *women's* clothes feature pre-pubescent *girls* (especially in swimsuits), models with anorectic bodies display clothes designed to make women into objects, and shop mannequins are literally shaved down each year to present the newest fashions on figures that correspond to fewer and fewer bodies.

Meanwhile women, not surprisingly, feel "oversized," too big in one part of their body or another, dissatisfied with particular features of their whole body as a "package." Bombarded by images of increasing slimness, women struggle to mirror the new image churned out seasonally. Trying on clothes in shop changing rooms, women judge themselves on how successfully they can reflect/reproduce the received images of femininity.

On one level it is a straight propaganda campaign coupled with the unavailability of stylish clothes in more than a few sizes—but the process is more insidious than that. Even women who have grown up with a reasonably healthy respect for their bodies (hard as this is to do in our culture) and who have not been previously preoccupied with body image are so assaulted with articles, advertisements, diet columns and advice on beauty matters that pedal thinness as a life solution that they find their confidence undermined. Feelings of dissatisfaction creep in, and few women under forty-five would see themselves as slim enough or their bodies as satisfactory. What was "acceptable" even ten years ago is now outsize. The Western obsession with slimness pushes women into a relentless struggle to press their bodies into smaller and smaller sizes. The beauty and variety of the female form are judged unacceptable, and instead slimness is promoted for profit and control.

As women are encouraged to become smaller and smaller and the Western obsession with health = slimness = happiness = diet intensifies, more and more books are rushed into the marketplace offering new, permanent weight-reduction schemes or advice on how to dress slim, minimize "bad points" and project the perfect body. Slimness, first marketed as a way to emulate the international jet set, has developed a life of its own. Success, beauty, wealth, love, sexuality and happiness are promoted as attached to and depending on slimness. Slimness instantly conveys these qualities as though they automatically go together like salt and pepper, gin and tonic, Saturday night and Sunday morning. In other words, slimness is made into a fetish and abstracted from what it is—just one particular body shape. Slimness sells women's bodies back to them, promising in its wake the good life. Of course, none of these marketed attributes are remotely connected to slimness, which stripped bare is nothing more than a fashion, a current ideal promoted for a variety of reasons that seem to depend for their persistence on a pervasive fear of women and a desire to package them safely into commodities.

Selling body insecurity to women (and increasingly to men too) is a vicious phenomenon. It relies on the social practices that shape a girl's growing up to make her receptive. Little girls are cautioned against touching and investigating their bodies. Similarly they are discouraged from using their body strength to explore the world. Young ladies' bodies, we learn, are to be kept clean, hair is to be kept tidy, sexuality is to be hidden and poise must be developed. Much of a girl's childhood consists of injunctions against physical expression and exploration. Too much ballet produces big calf muscles and a Charlie Chaplin walk, too much tennis makes one breast bigger than the other. These so called "wisdoms," transmitted from mothers to their daughters and from teenager to teenager, shape the way that girls feel about their bodies inside and out. They become inhibited and prey to the media persuasion that induces feelings of inadequacy at the same moment as it pretends to offer solutions.

This destabilizing campaign takes its toll on the daily lives, activities and aspirations of women. Slimness is believed to be the answer to difficult social and personal circumstances. Many a woman has described the solution to an unfortunate encounter, a disappointing weekend, a job not secured, a lousy day with the kids, a squabble with her husband, a low exam result, in terms of "if only I were slim" or "I'm going to lose weight this week." That women seek such a route is hardly surprising. That it is ineffective is a tragic comment on the complexities of how we are first robbed of our bodies and our access to many of life's activities and then thrust back on a narrow, individualistic non-solution—slimness.

Because of the pressure to be slim, many women who may not have had a history of eating problems in childhood or adolescence find themselves unwittingly interfering with the self-regulatory system that lets them know what, when and how much to eat. They disturb the mechanism of hunger and satisfaction signals and seek weight-loss schemes that actually initiate the diet-binge cycle. In moving away from internal cues to outside advice on diet, they inevitably try to reduce their food intake. This attempted reducing usually involves, in one scheme or another, the removal of certain types of foods from the woman's diet. In its place is put a scheme which depends on special food combinations of one kind or another.

There is always a new diet to try, always the possibility that *this* one will bring the accompaniments of happiness, success, love and health. But the schemes fail, for not only can't the diet deliver the goods, it becomes a jumping-off point for a cycle of deprivation that at some point—be it a day, a week, a month or even six months later—catapults into compulsive eating, bingeing and gorging.

Diets Turn Normal Eaters
Into People Who Are Afraid of Food

Diets rarely help a woman lose weight or reeducate her eating habits. Under the guise of control they bring havoc in the food area and frequently increased poundage. *Diets turn "normal eaters" into people who are afraid of food.* Food takes on all the punishing and magical qualities that anguish the compulsive eater. Our cultural obsession with slimness creates a whole new grouping of women who are unnecessarily drawn into having a food problem. As the women attempt to get slimmer, the diet organizations, diet books, exercise programs and so on get fatter and fatter on their pain.

This thin obsession that is inflicted on so many women makes it hard to resist the pressure to conform. Rebellion brings with it feelings of uneasiness and freakishness. It becomes quite difficult even to raise the question of *why* the massive variety that is woman's shape is systematically degraded; what is so awful and threatening about women's bodies at any size; why isn't fat considered attractive; why stature and fullness are devalued. Is the stigma that attaches to large or fat women not just another subtle way to divide one woman from another, thus promoting a false and individual solution to what should be at root a social concern—namely, the position of women in our society? Perhaps we can understand the impetus and energy behind the thinness campaign inflicted on so many women as a (possibly unconscious) skewed reaction to women's desires to be regarded seriously and take up more space.

Women look at each other and marvel at how older women manage to achieve "the look," "the face," "the body" that gives them a place and an acceptability in the world. Beauty and attractiveness are forever being redefined, but there still exists no place in the current equation for substantial bodies to be considered beautiful. The driven, induced need to be slim diverts us from concerns that are more truly central to our experience of life. It absorbs an energy that could help us change the world, not just our bodies.

A few brave women in western Europe and the United States are now battling against the prevailing standards, challenging them, turning them upside down, demanding rights for women of all shapes and sizes, classes and colors. But it is an uphill struggle punctured at every point by the hidden (and not so hidden) persuaders, reminding us that slimness is essential and that women must not occupy more than a little space.

CHAPTER 3

Food Awareness

What Is Compulsive Eating?

Compulsive eating means eating without regard to physical cues signalling hunger or satisfaction. It means, in fact, being so terribly out of touch with your body that these mechanisms are suppressed. Food is experienced as something almost magical, imbued with the power to make you feel better, to squash feelings, to provide comfort, to induce feelings of strength and so on. At the same time you may be fearful of food and what *it* can do, imagining that food is more powerful than the person who eats it, that it can do terrible things to you.

A compulsive eater feels out of control about what she eats. For some people that only happens at particular times, or comes and goes in waves. For other women, it is a constant battle. From time to time the compulsive eater will become inspired to "do" something about "it," by dieting, fasting, or trying to do away with the effects of the overeating by exercising, or taking diuretics and laxatives in large and dangerous quantities. Several times a week she will resolve to change the way she eats.

A woman frequently gets caught up in compulsive eating in the first place out of a desire to change her size because she *feels* too large. This desire to get smaller, thinner or slimmer then leads her to attempt to reduce her food intake. For many many women this desire is the trigger to a seesaw of food deprivation and bingeing. The deprivation can be more or less stringent, the bingeing more or less frequent and "extrav-agant." Women express these conflicts in a variety of ways, but there are four definite group types that I have observed.

There are those women who have been large for many years, who feel themselves to be fat, although they frequently underestimate their size, and who are quite despairing about ever being able to lose weight. They are frequently unaware of how much food they do eat and ex-perience their eating as somewhat chaotic. They discuss the topic quite openly and *feel that things would be a lot better for them if they were slim*.

The second group of women—by far the largest in number—are those who go up and down the scale (about a maximum range of sixty pounds). They diet from time to time and binge irregularly, though they overeat fairly consistently. They are quite open about talking about their food problems and *feel that things would be a lot better for them if they were slim*.

The third group of women are often average size, but weekly, daily, sometimes hourly, they binge on substantial amounts of food, which they then bring up. The name for this particular pattern is *bulimorexia*. Very few women in this group feel comfortable talking about their way of coping. They are fearful that disclosing how they are with food will result in a loss of control, or that they will be forced to give up their method of coping. They are desperate because they feel purging after gorging is the only way they *can* stay slim.

The fourth group of women are anorectic. They try to avoid eating as far as possible, and devise various schemes and regulations to limit what they do eat and then to rid themselves of the caloric value they've taken in. They often have a distorted view of their bodies, not realizing how very thin they are but instead seeing themselves as grotesque and enormous. Sometimes their control cracks and they binge (and some-times bring it up). They tend to be extremely closemouthed about their own eating but observe others closely. *They feel that things would be a lot better for them if only they were slim*.

When we look beneath the surface of these adaptations we can see that these ways of relating to food encompass much more than a desire to be slim. Their involvement with food stands for all sorts of com-munications that are unacknowledged. The way of being with food symbolizes a way of being with self, for example, harsh, punitive, inconsistent, depriving, angry, rebellious. Much self-dislike is sifted into the compulsive eating. It becomes a conveyor belt for the digestion, or rather indigestion, of uncomfortable emotional issues. In a broad sense a woman eating compulsively is absorbing the message of the culture and mirroring its relation to her. The world tells her she is unentitled and second class. She must love and nurture others with food but not herself. She develops a distorted relationship to food and her body. At the same time she is, in a painful and very personal way, using the food and her body to make a statement in the world. She is crying out for the kind of attention she knows so well how to give to others. She is trying to make a personal peace with the pressure to look a certain way. A confrontation is in process around food.

The Goal

The aim of this approach is to break the addiction to compulsive eating — to transform eating and mealtimes into pleasurable experiences that we can look forward to. This transformation can occur only if we move out of the torture and complications of the cycle of dieting, revolting against the diet, bingeing, intermittent overeating, feeling out of control around food and then taking ourselves by the scruff of the neck and recommitting ourselves to the deprived structure of the diet until once again we break it.

The method starts from the following points:

1. Compulsive eating is motivated by emotional factors.

2. Overeating occurs when a person feels unentitled to food and consequently is always trying to stop herself from eating. This self-denial goes hand in hand with its opposite, which is bingeing.

3. Compulsive eating and compulsive dieting are two sides of the same coin. The abstinence of one state explodes into the seeming chaos of the other. Dieting is *not* control: it is a stricture from outside imposed on the self. The control is vested outside us. Compulsive eating *feels* out of control, but in fact it originates inside us. For this reason, understanding unconscious processes can lead to greater harmony with our emotional needs.

4. Compulsive eating and compulsive dieting can be understood as addictions. They are serious problems requiring thoughtful interventions.

5. The psychological factors in compulsive eating relate to conscious and unconscious ideas of body image, i.e., "Who will I be slim?" "Who will I be fat?"
6. Compulsive eaters are out of tune with the body signals signifying hunger and satisfaction.
7. Women have a particularly complicated relationship to food because of the social meanings of food, feeding, fatness, thinness, dieting and femininity.
8. Compulsive eating and compulsive dieting are not disabling for life. They are not a chronic, incurable condition. They are an understandable response to psychological and social pressures.

How to Achieve the Goal: First Steps

Many women have found that the way out of the diet-binge cycle is to *stop dieting*. Review your eating/dieting history and see what your experience has been. Take time to do this, using a journal to write down what you find out about yourself. You may well discover that dieting did not work for you either as a way to "control" your appetite on a long-term basis, or to break your compulsive-eating patterns, or to help you stabilize at a weight that you want to be. You may come to the conclusion that dieting, rather than solving your food problems, added to them. Though a diet may often have looked like a good solution, perhaps it never actually worked out as it promised to. Now may be the time to take a leap of faith and stop dieting.

This can sound like an alarming idea, but consider it carefully. How many diets and weight-reducing schemes have you embarked on in your life? Is one diet really that different from any other? Don't they all lead eventually to your breaking the diet and eating in an out-of-control fashion, trying to make up for the period of forced deprivation? *Diets do not help you learn about your own bodily needs. They don't alert you to hunger and satisfaction; they don't break the compulsive-eating pattern.*

Identify Your Hunger

If you can give up the strictures of a diet, you can begin to approach your eating more sensitively. *Discover your times of hunger and what exactly you are hungry for.* Try to ignore all your mental restrictions on what you should and should not eat. Don't avoid foods you've always considered "bad"—junk food, desserts, chocolate, biscuits, potatoes or whatever. Focus instead on what you would most like to eat. Have it, taste it. Eat it slowly enough to taste it. See how much you want of it on this particular occasion. Now see if you can stop when you are satisfied. If you can develop a stance towards food that allows you to eat, you will more easily be able to stop when you've had enough. In other words, in giving up dieting and allowing yourself a free range of foods, you are opening yourself up to the possibility of *not* overeating.

Entitlement to Food

Because shame often accompanies being fat, and because in our culture there is so much pressure to deny ourselves food and become slim, many "overweight" compulsive eaters feel nervous about exposing that they want to eat. As a result, such women may often feel guilty about wanting to eat and may prefer to do so in private. Alternatively, they might try to conceal the kinds of foods they are eating so they don't experience the negative judgments of others. But this scheme rarely works out, since the woman feels such anxiety around food that she isn't really selecting carefully either when or what she wishes to eat. What *does* work is daring to break the taboo. Just because you're fat doesn't mean you have less right to food—or to anything else, for that matter—than other people.

Building Up Confidence

As you engage in this new process you will be building up a confidence that comes from satisfying yourself with food. You will be able to experience the sensation of hunger signals, and from that choose— without worrying about caloric values—the absolutely right food and drink that will meet whatever your particular appetite is at that time.

There are no recipes in this book, no menu suggestions, and no prescriptions as to when, what or how much to eat. Nobody can know better than you what feels and tastes right, what quantities match your appetite, what flavors will satisfy you.

Your eating behavior may seem somewhat strange as you try to be precise in meeting your physical desires. You may want little bits of food every few hours; you may discover that a variety of foods appeal to you and that you go through food phases; you may discover that your hunger corresponds to designated mealtimes. In all this you are the one who knows best what is right for you. Listen to your needs and then stick up for them by responding appropriately and without interference from "shoulds" or "must nots," good or bad foods.

As you eat the food you have chosen you will be able to enjoy it unambiguously—that is, without guilt or judgments. Because you have let yourself eat absolutely what you are wanting—and you know that this will be one of many, many such experiences with food, from now on—you will be able to stop when you are satisfied and afterwards feel the contentment that comes from looking after yourself with food in a precise way. For so many women with eating problems, guilt, physical discomfort, feelings of self-loathing, disrespect and recriminations are automatic accompaniments to any eating experience or even thoughts about wanting food. It is important to remember that in this therapeutic approach we are trying to break the compulsive-eating pattern so that food and meals are transformed from painful experiences into reliably satisfying ones.

You may wish to turn now to two exercises designed to help you find out more about your own psychological food constraints and aid you in trying to break through them. These are the "Ideal Kitchen" (page 131) and the "Supermarket" exercise (page 165). Allow yourself a good half an hour to do each exercise and then refer to the questions which follow it. You may wish to jot down your responses in your journal.

A Step at a Time

There can be infinite interruptions to the process of transforming food from a painful into a satisfying experience. Women eat compulsively for so many different reasons that, in the course of exploring why you do, there will doubtless be occasions when you find yourself eating more than you are wanting, grabbing for food or having mini-binges. These episodes do not mean the approach is not working, nor do they prove that you don't "deserve" to eat what you want any more. Each of these possibly upsetting experiences is in fact useful as a *clue* to help you unravel the mystery of your own particular eating pattern. Remember that you can use these experiences to help rather than punish yourself. The more you discover about yourself, the more possibilities there will be for you to intervene on your own behalf in a way that makes sense to you. Your various unconscious reasons for compulsive eating—or wanting to go back to dieting—will eventually come to light as you examine these kinds of incidents.

For example, Sara found that she frequently overate, just that little bit, whenever she had French toast. She enjoyed it so much that she couldn't stop herself. When she delved into why, she realized that she only made French toast once in a while and she was packing it in because she didn't know when she would be tasting it again. In a mini-version, she had set up a feast and famine relationship to the French toast. Once she saw what was going on she decided to make it more frequently. The result was that she didn't feel the urge to eat it so voraciously. She could stop when she was comfortably full, secure in the knowledge that she might make some again in a few days.

From Relaxation to Awareness

The aim of this approach is to encourage guilt-free eating so that you can really listen to what your body is wanting and give it the right kind and amount of food. However, I have learned from many women that what can happen initially is that the relief of being able to consider eating and food in a guilt-free way can be so enormous it can blind them to other aspects of their eating. In the effort not to judge every morsel that passes their lips, an amnesiac relaxation can occur when they eat. The permission to eat is translated into not knowing why or what they are eating. This may feel a lot different from the terrorizing voices that can accompany compulsive eating (as indeed it is), but if it continues for too long it can bring its own despair.

Often women tell me that they feel more relaxed around food but don't notice much change in their eating habits. What we then work on is how they can become more aware of what, when and how they are eating. Sometimes it can feel like a burden to have to concentrate on food, especially when you are trying to get away from being so obsessively involved, but in fact the only way to get through the obsession is to use it. Use it to observe your eating, gather as much information as you can, and then allow yourself to intervene differently. I am often pressed to remind women that the goal is to eat comfortably and with their hunger. The first step is to remove the guilt that surrounds all eating, but the next steps require more active engagement with the part of you that is struggling to eat in the new way. So from removal or reduction of guilt we move on to observe all the details of our eating behaviors.

Keeping a food chart is one way to find out more about your individual eating patterns. That food chart (on page 168) can be useful when you notice that you are somewhat glazed over about what your actual food intake has been and what the associated events, feelings and aftermath of eating experiences were like.

Observe in Detail

As you continue to observe your food intake you will probably notice that patterns emerge for you. For example, Clare noticed that she was really only comfortable when she was eating with her boyfriend or alone. When she wrote down her observations about having meals with others, she saw that she felt tense in a variety of ways. If it was a Chinese meal in which she was to share each dish with many people, she felt a certain anxiety that she would not be able to get what she wanted; either she would show herself to be greedy or she would hold back and feel deprived. This was in stark contrast to eating with her boyfriend Adam, with whom she could share quite comfortably. What she noticed was that with Adam she felt a confidence and security that she could have whatever she wanted. As happens with many couples, she went out of her way to give him the best of whatever was at the table and he went out of his way to give her the best. It wasn't that each was entitled to half—rather that in their relationship the meals expressed how they felt about each other, and since their concern for each other was in this case mutual, Clare could relax and feel reasonably sure that whatever she wanted she could have. There was never a hint of deprivation or worrying about appearing greedy. When Clare observed how she ate with other friends, where the sharing was based on an unspoken assumption of equal portions for each person, she noticed that the defined limit brought out her deprived feelings, and she felt she had to watch out that she didn't expose what felt to her like a desperation.

Clare decided to intervene and use this self-observation to explore the roots of her anxiety about eating with others. She began by choosing a restaurant where it was possible for her to have her own self-contained meal. This would allow her to eat with her friends without being under the pressure to share. In this way she might have more of a chance to find out what some of the underlying psychological reasons were for her desires to grab, without feeling she was acting them out in what felt to her like a humiliating way.

What she had to remember in the experiment was that when she was eating with Adam she ate with relish—and she usually ate less than at any other time. Clare needed to find out why this experience eluded her with others. She felt it must have something to do with emotional safety. What she discovered during the experiment was that when eating with friends she did not feel that they were really with her. Their attention was not focused on her but on the conversation or whatever else was happening. When it was focused on their interaction with her, Clare's eating was free of tension and she was able to eat leisurely and with enormous pleasure.

The issue that Clare had to confront for herself was: How could she help herself not to see others' actions as having directly to do with her? Why did she jump to the conclusion that something was being done to her (when people weren't riveted on her) rather than that she was affected by others whether their intentions were specifically focused on her or not?

When she looked back over her history she realized that when she was a little girl her mother was often distracted and only infrequently in Clare's memory did her mother pay specific attention to her around food. Of course, this information had long been obscured because so many of Clare's remembrances of her mother related to food and food preparation. Clare's mother, like most women of her generation, was responsible for feeding the family and spent much of her time in the kitchen and shopping for food. But she did not do this without having extremely complicated feelings. Some of these she hid from herself, because the times were such that it was hard for a woman to protest that aspect of her social role, but the impact of this forced service in the food arena meant that some of her ambivalent feelings spilled over into how she related to her daughter around food.

What had happened, from Clare's point of view, was that she did not have a secure sense of her mother's presence with her when she was eating. Because feeding is such an intimate communication in infancy and early childhood (since a child's survival is so dependent upon it), tremendous anxiety can arise when the child experiences her feeder as distanced or inconsistent. This is the memory that Clare had. She felt a richly secure and nourishing ambience with her mother but at other times felt a panic and fear that her mother was not attending.

This staccato pattern in her early relationship to food was psychologically jangling, and it was being replayed in her adult life in a more elaborated form. She had, unbeknownst to her conscious mind, projected on to Adam and her eating times with him that aspect of her mother that comforted and warmed her; on to her friends she had projected the distanced or withdrawn aspects of her mother, which induced anxiety in her.

With this insight Clare was able to take more responsibility for what she was actually doing. She could see that she grafted on to real situations emotional memories from her past. She struggled to trust that she could indeed allow *herself* to be engaged with herself when she was eating. She could be her own companion in that sense. She tried to sort through her feelings of insecurity and to acknowledge them more straightforwardly so that she need not express this issue through her food.

In fact, the painstaking psychological work she did in order to pinpoint what was going on for her not only freed her to work at the issues behind the eating—it also gave her a way to feel more secure within herself. Clare began to be able to see that as she allowed herself to pay more attention to her eating, she relaxed and enjoyed it. The good feelings she had experienced with Adam could now be taken into other settings. Unexpectedly, the new benefits regarding food made her realize how deeply tied she was to her mother and the never-ending conflicts that lived in that relationship. She began to feel an energy to work on their relationship unfettered by fears of food. This detailed analysis helped Clare find a new solution.

See if you can't piece together your own food pattern in a way that can open up new responses for you. Such observations may serve as a reminder to you that your compulsive eating has roots in your personal history. As you begin to understand those roots, remember that *each eating experience is a chance to change*. This means that every single day you will have one, two, three, five chances to intervene and not necessarily repeat that personal history.

Breaking the Binge Cycle

One of the dreaded aspects of bingeing is its cyclical nature. It starts with what feels like a mindless, driven stuffing down of food. This is followed by a feeling of being blotted out, stoned. The next morning, or a few hours later, when you have regained awareness and are perhaps feeling physically bloated, you are troubled by recriminations and you hope for the energy to make a new start.

Bingeing inevitably makes you feel you've blown it, and it takes a while until you feel able to put back on the straightjacket of the diet or whatever is your current regime for losing weight. Usually what follows is eventually another and yet another binge.

Giving up dieting does not mean that bingeing automatically disappears. It may well decrease and occur only sporadically, seemingly rearing its insistent desire out of nowhere. It may occur on specific occasions, around menstruation or when you feel particularly tense or disappointed. While you are working on the psychological motivations of your bingeing, you will need some practical down-to-earth steps with which to intervene in the binge cycle. Try following these the next time you are in a compulsive eating situation:

1. Sit down, slow down and take a moment to register that you are bingeing. Accept that you are bingeing—don't fight the impulse. Do you always go for a specific food during a binge? Are you tasting the food? Enjoying the food? If not, stop and ask yourself whether it is the right food. What do you *want* to eat?

2. Identify the feeling that led you to eat. What would be so terrible about having the feelings? Think about the emotional state you wish to achieve by eating. Is it oblivion? What do you want as an end result to the binge? What is your eating trying to express? What is your fat trying to tell people? What would be so difficult about facing these emotions if you were thin?

3. What will happen if you sit with your feelings? What are you exposing about yourself? Why is that so shameful?

4. See if you can experience your feelings directly, even if only for a minute or two.

Focusing in on your feelings, allowing yourself the breathing space to see what you really want, puts you in touch with your own power. It reminds you that *you*, not some outside or superimposed authority, are going to help yourself out. For a compulsive eater, the only way out of the pattern is to get inside yourself—to trust that there is a voice, a part of yourself, that can inform you about what you want emotionally and what you want from the food. This voice will tell you about a way to eat that will be uniquely yours. It will have specific aspects in common with other people's eating, but at its foundation it will depend on your own body's needs. Remember, nobody else can tell you what is right for you; nobody else can feel what is right for you. When you feel distraught after a binge, remind yourself to wait until you feel hungry before eating again and when that time comes listen hard, feed yourself and reflect on how that all felt. Feel the relief of being able to nourish yourself.

Sometimes it is impossible to intervene in a binge—you just can't tear yourself away from it, you are stuck on gorging and at the same time feeling upset by your actions. However, some relief may come from knowing that you can either break that particular binge or intervene in a future one. The very next time you experience hunger offers you the option of making a choice based on that hunger specifically.

If you are in the grip of a binge-hunger now, you may wish to turn to page 135 and see if the exercise on "Breaking Into a Binge" can be helpful.

How to Stop at Fullness

Knowing what fullness is and stopping at that point are often quite difficult for someone who has a long history of relying either on diets to guide her about quantities of food or on blow-up binges that have a final resting point. The satiation mechanism is a delicate one and, if it is abused continuously, may not be able to respond appropriately at first to the body cues signalling that you are full. Once food and eating become overloaded with emotional meaning, you may be out of touch with the body processes signalling satisfaction. The end of the cake may be where you stop habitually, rather than at the right amount for *your* body.

A good way to start to intervene is by pausing—that is, simply interrupting the sort of mindless overeating that seems to occur out of habit. If you can check in with yourself during every mealtime or snack, when you are halfway through whatever portion you have designated yourself, you can painlessly give yourself a rest and a chance to see whether indeed you wish to continue to eat. Often you will, especially if you aren't giving yourself portions that are consistently more than you are wanting. But you may discover that your body needs much less food than you ever imagined and that a full dinner is too much food if you are trying to be really in tune with your hunger.

You don't need to pause for a long time—perhaps just for a minute while you put down your knife and fork or spoon, or the chocolate bar, and reflect on whether you are beginning to feel satisfied and full. As long as this interruption is backed up by the right to continue to eat if you so wish, you may be able to get in tune with your body's wants.

Bear in mind that food takes an awfully long time to be digested. What you are searching for is a sensation in your stomach that, if you would but hear it, says: "Enough." Enough doesn't mean stuffed, it means walking away from the table contented, perhaps with room for "a little something else." It means sitting with *that feeling* for a while after finishing whatever you're eating, and checking twenty minutes or so later whether you might be wanting some more food or whether food per se has in fact slipped your mind.

Often just stopping requires a tremendous effort. You can be caught in the grip of an almost excruciating tension when you interrupt un-thought-out eating. When you make the decision to stop at a point when you feel full but still feel driven to go on eating, you may indeed experience a few agonizing moments of internal struggle. There is an intensity in that confrontation with yourself. The reassuring thing that you have to look forward to after those few minutes and that emotional hiccup have passed is the deeply satisfying feeling that comes from seeing yourself exert control rather than feeling controlled by the food.

Learning to recognize fullness is no mysterious process. At first you will need to be alert to the cues that your body sends out, but in time, after you have built up a repertoire of satisfying eating experiences, you will be able to stop as automatically as you did before you ever had a compulsive-eating problem. Trust your body to let you know when to start and when to stop.

It is much more difficult to stop eating if you aren't hungry for food when you start to eat. Your body will be incapable of giving you clues about satisfaction, only about bloatedness or discomfort, and you will find yourself frantically trying to limit yourself to "just one more slice," "just one half a portion," and having very little success. Nothing can be more unpredictable than the point at which a compulsive eater will stop eating if she isn't hungry when she starts.

Try to avoid this situation as much as possible by saying no to food when you aren't hungry. Don't be over-concerned about offending others. Switch your concern to where it belongs—your own food needs. Saying no to foods when you aren't hungry and not retreating from that decision can give you a tremendous sense of well-being. It is a mark of the fact that you are more consciously in harmony with your body. Every such experience builds up a memory of positive interaction with food. It shows you that *you can be appropriate* in this area *without depriving yourself.*

Some of the difficulty of breaking food addiction comes from not feeling confident that you can make lasting changes that will be more nurturing than eating compulsively. Since your goal is to develop a relaxed relationship to food, reminding yourself of how destabilizing it is to eat when you aren't hungry can help you make the choice *not* to do so, *not* to reiterate and act out the deep fear that you will never get through your food problem.

Leaving Food Over

As you tune in precisely with your bodily needs you are bound to have to confront the situation of leaving food on your plate at your own home, a friend's or in a restaurant. This can be extremely difficult, even when you are utterly full and you know that finishing everything is going to leave you feeling uncomfortable and stuffed, or not especially enjoying the food. These facts speak to how many emotional issues are tied up in eating, for if we just ate for enjoyment and the satisfaction of our physical needs, this dilemma would not arise. We would not experience conflict over refusing food or leaving some on the plate, or even turning it away.

Think about why this is so difficult in your case. Try, in different settings, leaving food over when you feel physically satisfied: first at home, then at a friend's, then in a restaurant. If it feels almost impossible, you might ask yourself the following questions (be sure to give yourself time to answer them):

1. Were you allowed to leave food on your plate as a child? If not, do you remember wanting to?

2. Do you feel you are offending someone by leaving food on your plate? Who will be offended?

3. Do you feel that this food is your last chance to eat?

Notice your feeling at the beginning of the exercise at the point when you are satisfied and are trying to leave whatever is left over on your plate. Get into the tension, experience its intensity and try to dissect it.

Try and sort out whether you feel you are offending others or whether you would feel too deprived yourself if you left it over. If it's a case of offending others, are you sure you really would be? Is it *everyone* you might offend, including the waiter or waitress, or is it just specific people, such as your mother, mother-in-law or a friend? Are you sure they still expect you, a grown woman, to finish everything on your plate? Perhaps your mother's attitude has changed now that she's seen you survive so well. Perhaps it would be okay not to eat everything she prepared for you.

If you imagine that you would feel deprived, are you sure that in fact you would? If you've enjoyed the food, you could choose to have the same again another time. What exactly would you be missing out on if you didn't finish the food? What are you frightened of not getting? Perhaps you could get what you really want from the situation or the other people without having to stuff down all the food.

Observe other people's eating habits. Look around you in cafes and restaurants and you will see how routinely people leave food on their plates. Nothing terrible happens to them. They survive till the next time they eat (and they do eat again!), and nobody else is really bothered one way or the other if there are leftovers.

If it feels more emotionally loaded than I have described (and I know this issue can be a very difficult one for many people), try and feel through what it is you think you are refusing in leaving food on your plate. Are you being rejecting? Do you feel disloyal? Are you expressing ingratitude? Are you wasteful? Are you spoiled? Try and pinpoint the feelings that are involved in this involuntary ingestion of food you really don't want, and see if the knowledge you gain doesn't help you break this pattern.

Risk Not Eating When You're Not Hungry

Related to being able to leave food on your plate is the ability to say no to food when you are not hungry for it. There are two different kinds of situations that can create a desire to eat when you are not hungry and, for those struggling to get over eating compulsively, special attentiveness and awareness is needed so that you can respond creatively. One type of situation occurs when you (or someone else) have been cooking: it's time to sit down for a meal and you have no appetite. The other situation is where we find ourselves going towards food—out of habit—when we aren't actually hungry.

In both these circumstances there will be times when you can intervene and not eat and other times when circumstances will make it very hard to do so. You may feel it necessary to explain to whomever has cooked for you that you just aren't hungry at that time, but that you are happy to sit with them while they eat. See if you can stay with the person or people and hold on to your decision. If you are about to eat out of habit, try putting off eating for a while. Not eating in these circumstances and observing your reactions will help you in the long run. Again, it will only be possible to do this without discomfort as long as you can be counted on to feed yourself exactly what you are wanting when you *are* hungry. Otherwise, passing up food will feel too much like deprivation.

Because these situations can crop up so frequently, I have designed an exercise especially to help you *not* eat when you aren't hungry. It's called "Increasing Your Food Awareness," and it begins on page 137. You may use it as often as necessary to help you increase your food awareness, clarify your emotional state and gain insight into your habitual eating patterns.

Theory into Practice

Some women have told me that they reach a certain level of understanding about their relationship to food and body image but do not find it easy to integrate their intellectual perspectives in such a way that it allows them to eat with more satisfaction. They may go through short periods of non-compulsive eating and then be even more disheartened when they find that they still go towards food when they aren't physically hungry. The question is often asked: How do I translate the theory into everyday practice?

My answer is as follows: eating is something we have an urge to do several times a day, and we have urges to eat for all sorts of reasons. Some stem from emotional needs that can't be met by the food and others arise when our body needs nourishment. At each desire to eat, we have a chance to put theory into practice—this means that several times a day we have the possibility of intervening in a creative way in relation to food. But it requires commitment, concentration and effort. It doesn't just happen.

When you notice that you want to eat, you can put theory into practice by *slowing down* and considering what and why you are wanting. Are you hungry? If so, what would you really like to eat? Is it available? How could you make it available? How much do you want? How is it tasting? Does it hit the spot? Stop and see whether it is as satisfying as you had anticipated. If not, think again. Perhaps you aren't really hungry. Perhaps the environment isn't quite right. *Check your reactions, slow down and give yourself the space to intervene.*

If you aren't hungry, what do you want? Stop and let yourself notice for a few minutes before you stuff down the response. Remember, this is a chance for you to understand something about yourself. *Don't expect this understanding to come without your attention.* Use the exercises on "Increasing Your Food Awareness" and on "Breaking Into a Binge" (pages 137 & 135).

Take a breather from your routine of feeling that *it* isn't working. See if you can remind yourself that you aren't physically hungry, and that therefore you might be able to go without food on this occasion. That doesn't mean you are depriving yourself. You are intervening in a new way, gradually putting theory into practice.

The experience will be stored in your memory and, if it is pleasant, you will be able to draw on it in a reassuring way in the future. If it is unpleasant you will need to go a step further and investigate what need you are asking the food to fill. What are you really hungry for? What kind of nourishment do you crave?

If you focus on this next level of questioning, you will develop new resources to use as part of the process of change. Be persistent in your attempts if you feel the understanding is there but the doing is terribly far away. It will come eventually.

But don't rush to make an insight happen. You may be forcing things too fast. Your fat and eating behavior are there for good reasons. They took years to cultivate. You may need time to assimilate new concepts and new possibilities. Don't berate yourself. Try to accept where you are right now. Above all, avoid the tendency to "victimize yourself" with "it doesn't work" or "it doesn't do it for me." Appreciate that you are involved in a struggle and that you need to find a balance within it.

This new approach may require a good deal of energy and this in itself may be irritating, for part of the attraction of this method is that it frees you of the obsessiveness associated with food and body image. This may present you with a short-term dilemma, but it will be in the service of your having a new and ultimately more satisfactory and relaxed relationship to food. Remember, you are working towards enjoying food and away from being so scared of it that you have to control or block yourself every time you eat.

CHAPTER 4

Food and Emotional Hungers

Individual Commitment

When you decide to work purposefully on your compulsive-eating problem, by yourself or in a group, you will need to make a commitment to yourself that is flexible enough to encompass the various moods, disappointments, and ups and downs you will go through during the process. You may feel exhilarated on first thinking about food, fatness and thinness in this new way. You will perhaps have an initial surge of energy and feel as though you are ready to conquer the problem once and for all. Experiences of non-compulsive eating will encourage this enthusiasm, so it may come as quite a letdown to discover that the problem does not disappear overnight or work itself out as easily as you may have hoped. You may feel discouraged just as you have in the past when another diet didn't work. You may often feel bored.

It is important to pay attention to this attitude and try to take a different stance towards it by making a different type of commitment to yourself. *It* won't work. *It* isn't an it. *It* isn't magic. *It* isn't even a dramatic solution. What you have is a compulsive-eating problem.

You can tackle your problem by engaging with it actively, by taking responsibility for yourself, your food struggles, your reactions to your body and your eating behavior. The problem rarely disappears on its own. Nobody else can solve it for you. If you are in a group with a leader, the leader cannot do it for you. *You have to do it yourself.* You can get help, assistance and support, but that is crucially different from hoping that others will take the responsibility for you.

You will need to do a certain kind of emotional work. This can be wide-ranging, including promising yourself to observe and identify the particular issues that are especially hard for you; weathering the rough patches when it feels as though nothing is changing; asking for things you think might be helpful to you from the people around you; reminding yourself that there are bound to be times when you take three steps forward and two steps back; being generous to yourself if you have a particular difficulty, without feeling as though you are being overindulgent or not engaging it; and so on.

Respect your own pace. Remember that you are seeking a fundamental change. Certain feelings or ideas that you hold as precious may shift, and that may be disconcerting, but allow yourself space to explore and work them through. At all costs, *don't expect to dispense with the problem in an inspired insight*. It might happen that way, but it most probably won't.

Be generous. You will be learning many important things about yourself during this process. One is that you *can* tolerate working things through. In your approach to this problem you don't have to reiterate the drama of success and failure, bingeing and dieting. You needn't be evangelical, just struggle to stay focused on your own issues.

Defining Oneself

Many women experience a fear of being defined, of drawing boundaries round themselves that then determine where they end and the rest of the world begins. We have grown up with the idea that our role is to be supportive, to help and give to others unselfishly. This requires that we ignore, suppress or sacrifice our own feelings and needs in the interests of those around us, particularly our families. Compulsive eating can often be a way of "blurring the edges" of our personalities, and being fat is often linked to feeling "big enough" to enclose and obliterate our own needs while still having extra capacity for meeting other people's emotional demands.

Behind these feelings of concern for others may lie a sense of desperation that our own needs are bound to be overlooked and would be impossible to meet in any case. For many women, both the actual and the imagined responsibilities we take on for others cut us off from our own deeply felt needs. At the same time, they can prevent us from taking a certain kind of responsibility for *ourselves*.

This dilemma needs to be grappled with, for it can be tremendously fulfilling to follow through a commitment to be responsible for ourselves in the area of food. Redrawing the boundaries is a step towards empowering ourselves. It fills us up in a nourishing way.

Being Opened Up to New Emotions

When you decide to look into your problems around eating and body image, you will be opening yourself up to a different relationship to your emotional life. You will be exploring issues that you may have wanted to avoid—indeed, the very point of the compulsive eating may have been to mask the issues or obscure the basis of any particular distress. For example, you may discover that you often find yourself eating compulsively when you are faced with a difficult decision—one that involves conflict. On your own or in a group you will be working towards understanding why decision-making and coping with conflict are so difficult for you.

Joan was the only daughter in a family of five sons. Her brothers had each gone to college, pursued the careers they wanted and married. She was the only unmarried child and had taken upon herself the responsibility for looking after her father when he was widowed. She spent much of her twenties making her life decisions based on his needs. As she approached her thirtieth birthday, she felt a tremendous urge to give up her well-paid job in advertising—for which she had just won an award—to take up a two-year course in creative writing at Iowa, 600 miles away from where she and her family lived. She felt very guilty and confused about whether she should be applying for the course, given her responsibility for her father; at the same time she felt in her heart of hearts it was the right thing for her. Her friends talked with her about her dilemma but it did not alleviate the guilt thinking about herself produced. She decided to let "fate" decide for her. She would apply for a scholarship. If she got it, she would then face the issue of whether or not to go, how to leave her job and what to do about her father.

Throughout this hiatus period, she was eating compulsively. She was scared to face decisions that might bring change and upset. She wanted to suppress all the disagreeable feelings that making a new decision stirred up in her. It turned out that her compulsive eating had the function of drawing her attention away from what she felt uneasy about—namely, facing making a decision—and diverted her attention instead into a familiar and somewhat more comfortable focus—food, fat and thinness. Joan brought up her eating problem in a compulsive-eating group and was surprised to discover that she actually had a problem with making a decision when it involved conflicting needs. She understood why she was eating in an "unthinking" way and her eating problem didn't feel so hopeless or incurable. She resolved to try and struggle with her newly discovered problem.

In order to have a new way to deal with this problem, you may find it helpful to remind yourself that you are embarked on an exploration. You will be engaging with aspects of yourself in a way that is new to you. It will inevitably stir up complicated feelings—many of them painful. It will help enormously if you can adopt an attitude of self-acceptance. Changing a deeply entrenched way of relating to yourself requires tenderness and compassion. You have been eating compulsively for substantial reasons. It won't just go away—you need to uncover its basis and then work towards finding a new solution.

Recognizing a difficulty such as that in Joan's case is in itself an important step towards breaking the pattern, for it is often the case that much of our energy is bound up in *masking* the difficulty. There may be shame, confusion, rage and upset associated with why decision-making involving conflict is such a problem. Once the allied feelings have a place to be expressed directly, they can lessen and give precedence to the critical issue that is there to be worked through. Realizing that you feel awful about being able to make a decision and that you often cope by eating compulsively begins to break the chain. The chain works as follows:

A difficult emotion occurs. This leads to some reaction of denial or repression that you come to feel bad about. In an attempt to stave off both the original difficult feeling and the associated feelings it throws up, you eat compulsively. This then leads to feelings of low self-esteem, anger, despair and so on about the compulsive eating. The original feeling that started the chain is displaced and seemingly uncontactable. You feel pain and alienation.

This confrontation with self is a critical feature of each person's work on compulsive eating. It is what will enable a separation to occur between difficult feelings and the usual response of eating. It won't be necessary to resolve the problem—in this case, the difficulty of making decisions that involve conflict—in order to stop eating compulsively, but it is crucial that the problem not be obscured and distorted in the process. If you are in a group, the group can help you hold and contain the problem, rather than hide it away.

I mention this particular example because it has come up so often. Many women experience tremendous difficulty facing conflict, whether it is in their job, community or relationships. It is part of our psychological development that we may experience conflict as so unbearable that actually living within the conflict seems an impossible option. Many women have discussed how they respond to this difficulty in two ways— either by not feeling able to be active at all in relation to an issue of conflict and being wracked by feelings of immobility; or by attempting to deny the conflict they feel inside by making a decision that does not feel right either. They have to deny the complexities of their reactions with a resolute stance because they experience the internal conflict as too painful. In other words, they draw a black-and-white picture and obscure the gray.

The activity of compulsive eating serves to stuff down and temporarily assuage difficult feelings. Now you will be working towards short-circuiting this pattern by looking behind the behavior to see what feelings are hiding. This process will require patience and sensitivity, for each person has a different pace and it is important to pay attention to your own emotional rhythm and allow it to emerge.

How to Sit with Emotional Issues

One of the most difficult issues each woman with a compulsive-eating problem may have to face in order to change the way she eats lies in how she relates to her emotional life. It may seem surprising to the compulsive eater that this is a problem at all, as she may experience herself as being emotionally expressive and open. But often the compulsive-eating activity itself is a response to and a substitute for all sorts of emotions. Compulsive eating may be hiding a painful store of emotions that a woman finds hard to accept in herself.

It may be that the compulsive eating exists to mask these emotions, that it acts as a stopper and stuffs feelings down. Or it may be that uncomfortable feelings become transformed in the course of compulsive eating so that whatever unpleasant emotions are experienced take the form of berating yourself for having overeaten.

In any work on emotions that you do, either on your own or in a group, it will be important to concentrate on emotional issues in a different way. Throughout our lives we receive specific injunctions about having or expressing particular feelings. For example, many women grow up with a taboo against showing anger. The taboo doesn't, however, successfully do away with angry feelings. Instead, such feelings become transported into more culturally acceptable forms such as women feeling depressed, or engaging in "nagging," or withdrawing, and so on. When we delve into some of the symbolic meanings of fat for individual women, we discover that it is frequently a way of showing anger.* The anger cannot be expressed directly and the woman unconsciously shows it through her body—she attempts to have the fat speak for her. At the same time she may stuff food down in a race to prevent the angry feelings from bursting out. If she weren't to eat compulsively when she experienced anger, she might feel overwhelmed with the unfamiliar feelings—that they will not stop, that they will propel her like the motor force behind a binge. Therefore an essential part of working through compulsive-eating problems involves building a new way of relating to emotional issues.

Distortion of painful emotions most often stems from the following three circumstances in our backgrounds:

1. We may have received injunctions against showing particular emotions.
2. We may have been discouraged from engaging in certain activities, e.g., initiating ones.
3. We may have felt emotionally rejected or misunderstood.

*For further discussion of anger and fat, you may want to refer to *Fat Is A Feminist Issue*, pp. 43–50.

Throughout the time we are growing up we pick up strong signals about what is acceptable. In order to fit in we eventually hide away the feelings that others find unacceptable. But this can lead to an incredible confusion and discomfort about such feelings, so that when they are touched they can be extremely raw and painful. This is often the process behind compulsive eating.

Linda has throughout her life received messages that her sad feelings aren't really to be shown to others. She walks around unaware of the fact that she, like everyone else, is subject to sad feelings. She knows she likes to go to a film and have a good cry over some sentimental plot, but in her everyday life she is cut off from her feelings of sadness.

However, Linda does eat compulsively, and when she gave herself some breathing space to explore the emotional issues behind several of her compulsive-eating episodes, she noticed (and indeed felt somewhat overwhelmed by) feelings of sadness. Preceding each compulsive-eating experience were sad things that touched her momentarily. Not knowing how to cope with these feelings, she converted them into eating compulsively and then felt awful about that. She moved rapidly away from one feeling into another more familiar one. She used the food as the mechanism, although logically the food couldn't possibly know what feeling it was supposed to take away. It couldn't know that its job was to prevent Linda from feeling sad.

The more she was able to break into her pattern of overeating and bingeing, the more space Linda was able to give herself to find out about her sad feelings. As she experienced them more they became less overwhelming. *They were experienced and then they passed.*

Food Cannot Banish Feelings

Linda discovered that in allowing herself to feel the sadness, she was filled up from the inside with something very real. She didn't feel hungry for food to fill a hole or a yearning that could never be satisfied. And this is perhaps the central point to grapple with in relationship to foods and moods: *food is incapable of making feelings go away; it cannot make things better, it cannot fill up whatever emptiness there is inside.*

All the involvement with food can do is to mask the processes of your inner life. At the end of each compulsive-eating experience you are still faced with whatever emotional turmoil existed to propel you into the eating. Feelings don't live in food. Food can provide *temporary* relief, and *that's all*. Compulsive eaters suffer because, instead of digesting an emotional experience and thereby integrating it, they interrupt the experience with eating and are left with undigested feelings.

Making Space for Feelings

Linda used the information she gained to try to intercept a binge while it was happening. In order to do this she gave herself several options. First she decided to stop eating. She then tried to locate anything that might have led her to feel sad. Sometimes she was able to contact those feelings and sometimes she wasn't.

On those occasions when she was able to pinpoint an incident that brought up sad feelings in her, she then had a further choice. She could either give herself some space to experience the feelings and to work out what pained her, or she could decide to ignore the feelings.

Ignoring them did not mean resuming eating compulsively. It meant identifying the feeling that was leading her to eat. This kind of intervention allowed a shift in the way she ate. She might find herself eating compulsively, but she had a choice whether to continue.

Why One Binges

Eating compulsively and then obsessing about it has a function. It removes you from the immediate confrontation with whatever is causing you so much pain. Although the obsession cannot solve the problem but only postpones an honest look at what is going on, it can provide relief in a short-term way by removing you from the source of the pain. A binge is predictable. You are familiar with the course it takes. It leads you through a pattern of emotional responses that you have come to know, and it allows you to temporarily absent yourself from what is going on in your environment that is causing the distress. Difficult emotions can be postponed and transformed into a form that is knowable—a binge. There are few surprises in a binge, as they almost always follow the same pattern for each individual (although the pattern varies from individual to individual).

If you are anguished about not having a close personal relationship, you might find yourself having a binge. In the course of overeating, you will make the food and your fat the reason why you aren't having the kind of intimate relationship you long for. As the binge continues the food provides a bit of comfort while your mind proceeds along the following lines: if I weren't bingeing, if I weren't fat, I could be in a relationship. As it is, I'm not and I feel bad about it, but it is in my power to change the circumstances if I were just to stop eating.

Now of course this reasoning has both some truth to it and some falseness. We cannot control very much outside of ourselves. We can't as individuals make the world turn out the way we want it to. But this is a humbling idea that most of us, because of the way we have been raised, find hard to accept. We want to be able to have a decisive impact—we want to be able to make things happen. Giving yourself a reason that you seemingly have control over is an attempt to justify things to yourself internally.

The tragedy lies in the fact that the obsession can take up the energy that you might use to affect things in so far as you *are* able. Obviously all of the reasons do not lie in your hands as to whether or not you have a close relationship, but some of them do. Not looking at what you can actually do to affect things means living with a kind of uncertainty and risk-taking. Choosing overeating and obsessing as an option can feel safer.

The problem is that this doesn't address the anguish that we carry around inside. It substitutes a self-contained obsession for an engagement with the problem. Moreover, no particular food can respond precisely enough. It cannot meet the feelings appropriately. It doesn't know what to give you. The food doesn't know whether to quash anger or hurt, disappointment, sadness, conflict, fear, insecurity, guilt or whatever. A person who is engaged in compulsive eating is actually giving the food the power that they themselves own to suppress uncomfortable emotion. The Mars bar does not have written on it: this will make Sally feel less angry; this will make Jane feel less guilty; this will make Sandra feel less chaotic.

Emotions such as these, that trigger the compulsive eating,   ❋
are ultimately knowable. At first they may seem mysterious, perhaps even ridiculous, but as you devote more energy to exploring them you will come up with emotional explanations for your compulsive eating that make sense in your guts. The exercises on "Exploring Your Feelings" and on "Expressing Your Feelings," which you will find on page 143, and on page 141, will help you explore, acknowledge and express your uncomfortable feelings. Use it as often as you wish.

If you feel incapable of coping with such emotional turmoil, remember this simple point: you are already cutting off the feeling. The food isn't doing it for you. Therefore you don't need the food to do it. The food is just a conveyor belt, from you to you, that allows you to cut off the feeling. You could eliminate the taking in of the food without eliminating its purpose.

If you don't feel at a particular moment that you can cope with a distressing feeling, it is all right not to. Ask the Mars bar what kind of feeling you were wanting it to suppress. Inquire of it what kind of feeling you were wanting it to give you. Then see if you can reach that state without it. If you are trying to break through your food obsession, you may not feel comfortable being flooded by so many emotions. You can certainly control the flow. Sometimes try to experience the feelings directly, at other times acknowledge that they are there but do not allow yourself to be swamped by them.

Feelings Are There to Be Experienced—Not Solved

Many women say that once they discover they are eating compulsively for emotional reasons they then don't know what to do about the emotions they are uncovering. But there isn't anything to *do* about emotions, except to recognize them. They aren't objects or monsters—they are part of you, even the dreadfully painful ones. But they can feel *not* part of you if they have been hidden away and denied for years. They can feel unmanageable and disruptive. In fact you have been carrying them around in a distorted form and thus they have rarely had a chance to come to the surface, be experienced and find their own level.

If, for example, you discover that you eat compulsively to cover terrible hurts that you don't want to look at, it may come as something of a relief to experience the hurts rather than being bound up in suppressing them. They are past hurts that you unconsciously pushed aside because you didn't have the resources to deal with them when they occurred. But you aren't in the same kind of vulnerable position now that you were in when you were very young. You don't need to rely on others in exactly the same way that you once did. If you allow the feelings to come to the surface and perhaps find yourself tearful, you are not likely to be scolded for being silly. You may not feel sufficiently understood if you try to explain what you are experiencing to someone else, but you will not be humiliated in the same way that you were when the original hurt occurred.

We can't help but project on to our present the emotional melodies of our past, but it is important to remember that we will not necessarily be met with the same kinds of responses. Our vulnerable areas may not upset those we are close to now in the same way they affected those we were close to when we were little. If you tell a friend you are miserable, she may be more likely to listen or perhaps try to cheer you up than were your parents, who felt more identified with you and subsequently were often less able to hear your pain.

Parents and children are often entwined with one another in such a way that the parent can feel guilty or upset on the child's behalf rather than giving her the space to live through her own upset. Friends are not merged in the same way. They can feel an empathy that does not necessarily bring up feelings that either it is their fault or they must do something to make you feel better immediately.

Feelings aren't there to be solved, but to be experienced. As you can allow yourself to have your feelings, they will become less frightening. You will be developing confidence that you can have more direct contact with your inner life and not have to cut it off by obsessing about other things or by eating compulsively.

CHAPTER 5

Body Image

How to Improve Your Self-Image

In our work on compulsive eating we take as a starting point the assumption that most women feel uncomfortable with and in their bodies, whatever their size and weight. Women feel insecure and frequently reach out to body transformation as a cure-all for other issues. The perpetual enticements of the "slim body" merchants mean that tremendous strength must be exercised in order to look afresh at our bodies and try to see them for what they are.

If they are fat, that may well be a statement of self-dislike, a desire to be distinguished from the crowd, a test, a rebellion. It is not just one thing and it isn't the same for everyone. It may be that feeling or being fat so upsets us that we hate our bodies and feel despair about taking care of them.

Finding out for yourself what your "fat" is expressing—need? anger? loneliness? emotional hunger? protection? substance?—allows a new relationship to your body. As you can understand its language you can get a better sense of it. You may be able to notice what you really look like rather than living in a condemned cell flooded with seemingly relentless negative self-judgments.

The "Fat/Thin" exercise on pages 145–148 is designed to elicit the many feelings and associations we attach to body size. Don't

63

be surprised if you find contradictory or negative associations emerging. You may discover that fatness is not only felt as negative, but also has positive connotations. You may contact feelings about the "thin" you that are unpleasant, as well as those that are pleasant. It is important that these ideas—which you hold preconsciously and are not generally aware of—are brought out into the open so that you can explore them and grapple with their meanings.

In *Fat Is A Feminist Issue* I discussed the importance of familiarizing yourself with the conflicts and symbolic meanings that are part and parcel of body-image states. The more you get to know about who you are and what you are asking the various body states to convey for you, the quicker you will be able to work through the barriers that prevent you from being your ideal size.

So many times when a woman looks at herself, it is as though a tape full of self-denigration is turned on. She feels wrong. Her image in the mirror does not reflect what she would like. She doesn't look like Jane Fonda, Diana Ross, Sophia Loren and so on. Look again.

Try to open your eyes wide enough to see yourself, who *you* are. Imagine being more *you* than you are, rather than more somebody else. What would that mean? How would you look? How would you hold your body if you didn't disapprove of it? How would you walk? How might you sit? How would you stand? How might you dress? What would being comfortable in your body *feel* like? See if you can imagine it. Don't zoom to pictures of past or instant thinness. They could only have felt precarious in their own way.

Concentrate on yourself. What do you see? Look from the outside in and then try to feel your body from the inside out. Think of the functions of your different body parts. Are hands merely for decoration or are they moving, active parts of us? Are legs for adornment or do they serve important other functions? Try and see the wealth of activities that your body performs and is capable of; try and appreciate its physicality and adeptness.

Now think through how often you judge your body, censor yourself for what you put in it, thus creating a spiralling self-loathing. What pose do you slump into when you have these thoughts? Look at yourself and allow yourself the possibility of enjoying your body, of learning to appreciate it rather than castigating yourself. Be as *you* in your body as you can and try to project that feeling as you go about your daily life.

This is often difficult to do. However, it can be extremely useful for helping you move on from self-loathing to a more accepting attitude towards yourself. It is almost impossible to get rid of something you cannot bear to look at in the first place. You can't lose something that doesn't belong to you. Thus until you accept the way you look now, you won't be able to change.

To work on this aspect of body image, turn to the "Mirror Work" exercise on pages 149–151. Put a chair in front of a full-length mirror, and make sure you won't be disturbed for twenty minutes or so.

First Thing in the Morning

Often our dreadful feelings about our bodies come over us almost from the moment we wake up. Before we have had a chance to approach the day, we are disabled by self-loathing. To try to break into this painful pattern, imagine as you are waking up that you have a body worthy of respect and appreciation. For just a moment give yourself a breather from the judgments. Lie back in bed and look down at your toes, your feet and your ankles, gradually working your way up as far as you can see, and then feel your head perched on your shoulders. Now instruct yourself to imagine that you are contented with your body. Lie back, close your eyes and think about your activities over the next half hour. Plan what you will do: shower? dress? breakfast? Bear in mind your newfound pleasure in your body.

Now get up and involve yourself in these selected activities, all the while holding on to the idea that you like your body. Soap it with affection, dress it with care, feed it with just what it is wanting. See what a difference having a positive self-image makes. Stay with these good feelings for as long as you can during the day. Make a plan to remind yourself every hour of your experiment. It is very easy to fall back into a sort of mindless self-disapproval, but for one day try and take a different view towards yourself.

Experiencing yourself in new ways will provide you with a break in your routine of self-judging. At first, experiments like this may feel somewhat contrived and artificial, but their function is to provide stepping stones to a more harmonious self-image. You are bound to stumble on important insights that you can use as you make the journey towards greater self-acceptance. As with all that I suggest in this book, approach yourself with compassion and tenderness in order to build your self-esteem.

Fear of Being Your Ideal Size

One of the problems that can come up when you increase your awareness about food is the need to recognize the conflict you feel about being your fantasized ideal size. I have noticed during the course of therapy, as some women begin to eat in a more truly nourishing way, that, although they are initially delighted at their capacity to eat in this new way, they suddenly find themselves becoming preoccupied with how they look and their body size, and they can feel as desperate as ever about wanting to lose weight.

When we explore what is going on more deeply, we often discover that the worry about size is acting as a sort of bludgeon—almost as though it is preventing the new changes that are occurring from being consolidated. It's like a needle of insecurity that serves to undermine the good feelings that were building up from the positive eating experiences. It is terribly distressing to the woman involved but it can be an important message to her too, alerting her to look into aspects of her relationship to food, fatness and thinness with which she hasn't yet come to grips. Jessica came to therapy when she was twenty-two years old, having felt herself to be out of control around food and full of upset about her body size since puberty. When I met her she wanted to learn how to eat differently and to reach a size that she felt more truly expressed who she was. This was a size she had dieted to many times before, lived at for a week or two and then retreated from.

After several months of therapy she was having continuous experiences of feeling comfortable around food. Released from dieting and deprivation, she rarely binged and found that, as she was tasting food rather than shovelling it in, she was much more selective about what appealed to her. Her eating became a source of pleasure and a time to give herself a particularly nice kind of attention.

However, Jessica found that she was eating just that bit more than she really wanted on every occasion when she sat down to a meal. She had lost the food obsession per se but was caught in a tug of war trying to reach her goal size and continually retreating from it. As the pattern persisted it became obvious that the focus of the psychological work she needed to do should be on the meaning of her desire to reach her ideal size and the fact of her clinging on to a larger one. The actual weight difference in her case was not very marked (ten to fifteen pounds), but the fear associated with being her ideal size served to make her feel uncomfortable and rejecting of who she was on a daily basis.

She then concentrated on what thinness and non-thinness meant to her. She reviewed in detail her previous experiences of changes in body size. She discovered in herself feelings of precariousness and frailty when she felt herself to be slim. She felt diminished and scared that she would have achieved something she had to keep up. She realized that her current size somehow gave her the leeway to be more herself— she didn't always feel on top of things, she felt comfortable with a certain fuzziness around the edges, she felt she was somewhat scatty and liked that about herself. She felt that her ideal size presented her as more angular and purposeful than she felt herself to be. She had enormous difficulty detaching these emotional issues from the body states she had assigned to them and would frequently interpret situations in such a way that body image became an explanation and a vehicle for emotional expression.

At that time Jessica became ill with pneumonia and her dilemma about body size was dramatically back on her agenda. As part of her illness she lost weight and became frail, weak and vulnerable. The very feelings that she had feared emerged in the illness, but with a result that perhaps she would not have anticipated. Recovering from the pneumonia and getting her strength back showed her that she could be slim and survive. She did not undergo a personality change through being physically weak or because she lost weight. She was every bit herself and just as reassuringly scatty.

Jessica reached her slim state by a rather unfortunate route, but once having reached it she demystified it for herself. It is my belief that with or without the pneumonia she would have in time risked being at her idealized size to find out what it actually held for her. She could then have worked through which size felt more comfortable when all was said and done.

If your experience of teetering between two body images is similar, you might try following the steps that Jessica took and use her experience to learn and experiment with yourself. Obviously you do not need to become ill in order to stabilize—even if just for the course of the experiment—at a lower weight.

Do the exercise on "Fat/Thin" (pages 145–148) and try to   ❊
specify what various body images mean to you.

1. Try to detach the body states from the emotional issues.
2. Explore the emotional issues in their own right.
3. Experiment with the different sizes. Do they actually conform to what you imagined?

If slimness is what you desperately feel you want, then eat with close attention, allow yourself to reach that size and see how it feels. If you don't like it, try and pinpoint why. If it feels not like you and not like a you that you will get accustomed to, you can always allow a truer size for you to emerge. Just because you experiment with slimness doesn't mean you have to stay in it if it doesn't feel good. Doing the "Fat/Thin" exercise on a regular basis is extremely useful. You will discover that slimness means different things to you from the vantage points of different actual body weights. Remember, slimness is not a panacea, it was just sold to you as such, and once having succeeded in becoming slim you may feel able to reject it with strength rather than out of feelings of inadequacy.

Living in the Here and Now

Many women have faced the problem of feeling impatience that their body is not changing as fast as they would like it to. They resent that this method involves a process instead of producing instant change. While the slowness of this method does have significant advantages in that it allows you to explore the feelings that accompany different body sizes, the way down or the ups and downs in size that can occur can be frustrating. As comfort I can only say that perseverance does pay off. Experiencing different body sizes and getting used to them will be useful in the long run. The body size you decide to stabilize at will have more certainty in it and you will have developed confidence and self-acceptance in the process.

Each body size has something to teach you and has a validity of its own. Self-acceptance, a key goal, can be achieved if you can give yourself the permission to live in the here and now at whatever size you are. Just because you desire to change your body size should not preclude you from treating yourself well whatever your current size. Living in the present and inside your body means ceasing to torture yourself, making the effort to be as imaginative with your clothes as you can be and not excluding yourself from activities because you are "too big."

Largeness should not exclude you from loving, eating, dancing, swimming, running or involving yourself in the millions of activities you have put on the back burner until the slim you arrives. Life doesn't start with slimness or stop at anything larger. Life is for living with as few personal impediments as possible.

Goodness knows we are channelled into one route or another in hundreds of different ways because of the rules of the society we grew up and live in. The external constrictions can get under our skins in extremely complicated ways, and we may choose to use our energy to try to change the conditions of our lives that oppress us. But a part of that struggle involves being able to maximize the power we have in shaping aspects of our lives at a very personal level.

For a woman to take pride in her body for herself, rather than as an instrument or as an object, is a radical act. For women to proclaim that comfort and pride at whatever size they may be creates a chink in the armor of a patriarchal order. Taking this stance is difficult and hard to do on our own. But as more women reject the stereotype of driven slimness and exhibit a pleasure in women's physical variety, individual women can draw on that collective strength to build acceptance and confidence.

Self-hatred focused on body image is both painful and in the end dysfunctional. It rarely motivates anyone to change permanently, to lose weight and feel good. If your particular wish is to become smaller, start off with where you are now. Give yourself a bit of a breather. Direct the energy that is harnessed in self-loathing in a new direction.

Try accepting who you are at this very moment, not who you will be ten, twenty, thirty, forty or fifty pounds from now. Life does not have to be postponed until the day slimness arrives. It can be engaged with actively right now, whatever size you are.

If you can follow this prescription, the odds of your reaching the right size for you and staying there are measurably increased. If you are living for now every day and not postponing or restricting activities to when you plan to be slim, you will feel less precarious when your thin self emerges. It won't be a big unknown, a body size all tangled up with complex emotions. It will just be a new body size that you've been preparing for and that is organically you.

Beyond feeling too large or too fat in general, almost every ❄ woman has a part of her body that she is prone to focus on, seeing it as too fat or otherwise unacceptable in one way or another. If you do the exercise on page 153, entitled "Part of the Body," you may gain some insight into the various emotional issues that you've invested in a particular body part. You may be able to determine any distortions you have and thus feel some relief. If there are several parts of your body that especially bother you—let's say you've deemed your thighs and your breasts unacceptable—do the exercise twice, focusing first on one part and then on the other.

Pregnancy and a New Infant

For women who are struggling to find a comfortable relationship with their bodies, pregnancy can be a time of continuing shifts in how they relate to themselves. Some women enter pregnancy with their food problems mostly worked through but with twinges about how their new state might affect their eating and body image. Others become pregnant before their compulsive-eating problem is resolved and have to cope with complicated feelings of lack and loss of control of their bodies.

Many women have observed how being pregnant forced them to focus on their bodies in new and exciting ways. The changes that each trimester brought, the daily changes and new physical sensations and emotional states coupled with the desire to provide the healthiest possible environment for the baby growing inside of them, produced a heightened awareness of what they were eating and how they were holding their bodies.

Many women have reported that, after the initial confusion during the first three months as to what their food needs were, they settled into a pattern of feeding themselves and caring for themselves that felt easy and good. Their bodies were changing beyond their control but in reliably predictable ways. They were feeling good within themselves and were the recipients of much attention, concern and approval from others for being in the pregnant state. Having a tummy was for the first time legitimate and praised. People used different words to describe these body changes than those associated with fatness. They effortlessly found ways to compliment the new growth, thus giving the lie to the "fact" that only slimness can be beautiful. So for many women the experience of pregnancy brought unexpected side benefits.

The arrival of the new infant, and the profound changes this event ushered in, affected women whom I've worked with in different ways. For some, the experience of mothering in a supportive environment, their enchantment with the child and their pleasure in the intimacy shared in the feeding relationship allowed the women to enjoy the postpartum changes in their bodies and to settle at a size that felt comfortable and right. The importance of responding appropriately to the new infant's food needs spilled over into a consciousness of their own food requirements.

For others, the loss of the fetus inside of them and the reality of what it meant to be with a baby, with all the attention now riveted on the new arrival, brought up in them feelings of loss of identity, confusion about boundaries and of being somehow cast aside. They experienced others' concern for them mingled with a focus on when they "would get their bodies back." The sheer exhaustion of being up all night with a newborn, providing so much nurturance and having little sense of separation, led them to eat when not hungry in an attempt to give something to themselves. In moments of frustration, when perhaps what they needed was a rant or a hug, food was accessible and comforting.

Still other women found the shift from breast- or bottle-feeding to spoon-feeding difficult. In bottle- or breast-feeding they had found that their babies could send out cues that they were physically satisfied, and the infants could perhaps rest at the breast, not requiring food but

enjoying the comfort. Spoon-feeding removed the give and take somewhat and provided for less discreet discerning on the mother's part.
Feeding times became more tense and mothers found themselves agi-
tated over whether the baby was getting enough food, only to find they
were no longer being as self-discriminating about their *own* food as
they desired. If pre-pregnancy clothes did not fit, some women found
it hard to take the time or the money to find comfortable alternatives.
They became involved in a process of ignoring their own needs and by
so doing effectively disowning their bodies. In those instances where
regular sexual relations for one reason or another had not resumed after
the arrival of the baby, the feelings of being distanced from their bodies
were reinforced.

As these different dynamics—and of course, as people are individuals there are as many variations on them as there are mothers—were
recognized, the women felt strengthened in their attempts to reintroduce
themselves to their bodies. One working woman was pleased to return
to her job and the identity and purpose it gave her. She felt that profes-
sionally people were relating to her almost as they had before. People
valued her for her accomplishments, not only in terms of her mothering
qualities. She appreciated the division between her home life and her
work life, and this separation helped her become more defining again
in regard to her body.

As babies become toddlers and begin to show more independence,
that too can bring up changes in how a woman expresses her body
image. If her child's passage through early childhood evokes in the
mother echoes of her own early life, she may find herself over-iden-
tifying with the child, psychologically merged so to speak, and expressing this through a body change that indicates her lack of boundaries
and self-definition.

The cyclical nature of the mother-daughter relationship, through
which, in turn, the girl grows up to be a woman like her mother, can
trigger off in the mother extraordinarily complex feelings. Women have
talked about how their adolescent daughters' developing sexuality stirred
up feelings in them they found hard to handle, and how in some cases
they almost abdicated their own sexuality to become the protectors of
their daughters. Previously modish women have been startled to find
themselves "spreading" and dressing in a matronly fashion, or con-

versely competing quite unconsciously with their daughters and losing a sense of their own age, shape and appropriate body image. This is not to alarm those embarked on motherhood but to alert the readers to the kinds of issues I have come across and the vulnerability that can create difficulties for women at different stages of their lives in relation to body image.

Only twenty years ago, mothers of teenagers looked like "mothers," middle-aged and somewhat straightlaced. A flashy mother was exceptional and attracted comment. But with today's stress on "youthful" images, which means slimness and fashion consciousness for all, women's bodies do not necessarily go into hiding after the age of forty, and the old rules now conflict with expectations. Motherhood can thus be an extremely confusing time for women, and this can be expressed through their self-image.

CHAPTER 6

Exploring Your Problem

Helping Yourself

Self-help is a challenge. It is uncharted territory for everyone, and whatever happens for you as an individual (or as part of a group) will be unique. Many people are awed by the idea of self-help therapy. They may worry that, without therapy skills or a leader, they will do the wrong thing. People often feel hesitant about knowing how to help themselves or each other and may feel unsure about any interventions they might make. These concerns are understandable because obviously it feels hard to ask yourself, or someone else, the very questions you might have been running away from about your relationship to food, fatness and thinness.

However, this is also precisely the strength of the method, whether you are trying to sort through your compulsive eating on your own, as a pair or in a small group. For the questions you are afraid to ask may also be the ones that are most helpful. Once having given yourself permission to focus in on this area in a new way, you are already on the road to engaging with those very questions.

Choose a pace that feels right for you. In setting aside time to look at the issues involved in your compulsive eating, the possibility opens up that understanding, tninking, feeling and being compassionate towards yourself can give you more than dieting and deprivation. So often for compulsive eaters the first and virtually automatic response to a feeling or an event is to eat. Here we are clearing space for a special time to explore those impulses and to find new ways of coping with them.

Before working on the psychological level, many practical issues must be sorted out. If you are thinking of starting or joining a group, please refer to Chapter 7, "Organizing a Compulsive-Eating Group," before plunging in here. In *Fat Is A Feminist Issue* (pages 128–62) I discussed how I thought it was helpful to structure a compulsive-eaters group. In this section I will also suggest ways of working alone or in pairs that will help you explore your feelings within a safe and supportive framework.

First, however, it must be acknowledged that it is hard for many of us to take the time on a regular basis actually to focus on our own needs. You can have all sorts of good intentions that you'll go swimming each week, keep your room tidy or answer letters promptly, or whatever. Sooner or later these schemes break down and it can be ages before you are able to make a new resolution. In working with yourself on your compulsive eating, you will probably find it quite easy to start off with energy and enthusiasm while at the back of your mind you still feel wary about when you will let yourself down again. I think it is quite important to recognize this dynamic so that you can take it into account and not be depressed by it.

If it is realistic to spend ten minutes a day reflecting on your food problem, do it that way. Use five minutes to review your eating and another five to think through the difficult emotional issues that came up for you. If it is more realistic to spend an hour every four days reflecting on these themes, then choose that method. Using the exercises can help to focus your mind and energies, so allow time to do them *and* to note your responses. Be as flexible as you can, knowing who you are and what is likely to work for you. If you find you are not scheduling special time to think things through, then apportion a little time after each meal to digest not just the food, but your emotional relationship to it.

But *don't be totally casual about this time*. However and whenever you plan it, make sure you have quiet space to yourself. Take the telephone off the receiver or settle the children down to bed first if that is what it takes to guarantee that you are not interrupted. Have a notebook handy to jot down your thoughts, or speak aloud into a tape recorder and listen back to yourself. Take yourself and your work on compulsive eating seriously and make sure you spend purposeful time with yourself. Allow yourself the time and space to come to grips with the problem. As I have said before, this method depends entirely on *your* willingness to allow it to work for you. The way to start, after having assured yourself of some uninterrupted time, is by thinking, feeling, talking things out and reviewing your experiences of eating in a purposeful way.

Co-counselling: Learning to Listen and Learning to Talk

Co-counselling is a good vehicle for talking in pairs about emotional issues. In this method, two women take turns talking and listening to each other for a set period of time. The idea is to offer each other reciprocal help. The talker, who sits facing the listener, is aiming to say what is on her mind. The job of the listener is to *be attentive*—not to intervene—to listen to what the talker is saying and allow herself to feel with the talker the incidents and feelings she is describing. After an agreed amount of time (usually between seven and fifteen minutes) the talker and listener exchange roles for an equal length of time.

You decide what you want to work on, and how. You might find yourself talking about your current difficulty around eating, or how hard it was for you to attend your session because you were feeling discouraged. If you are in a compulsive-eaters group, you might use a short co-counselling exercise to sort through what you will eventually discuss during your time in the group. Often what is uppermost in our minds turns out to be less important to us than we think it is, and by talking we discover that our immediate concerns mask something more central to us.

It could also be that simply being able to say what is on our mind resonates and makes us realize just how important that particular issue is. In fact, you can use co-counselling to learn how to talk in a very different way for—unlike conversation in which people agree, disagree, interrupt, intervene, encourage and so on—you will be on your own, having to tap into what is really central for you using whatever words express what you really feel.

As you are talking you will be developing a new voice, a voice that is authentic. Because there will be space around your words, you will simultaneously be able to be reflective. This is quite a unique experience. Even if you are working on your own, you can adapt this method by speaking into a tape recorder and listening to yourself attentively afterwards.

For the listener, too, this will be a new experience. For in that capacity, you will be developing your skills as a listener; learning to give attention to another person without interrupting her space; learning to understand things from the other person's point of view; learning to get inside her experience and out of your own. This listening skill is of enormous importance if you join a group, where you will be trying to pay special attention to the words, feelings and interactions of other group members.

After a period in which you have each had a chance to talk and a chance to be listened to, I suggest you sit silently for a minute or so to reflect on what you have noticed. Then give each other feedback about your experience of yourselves and of each other. If you try a short period of co-counselling in pairs at the beginning of a larger group meeting, use the time to find out what you want to work on later, and how you're feeling. Often what you will be confronting in these co-counselling sessions are difficult, painful, confusing and sometimes incomprehensible feelings. Listen to yourself with the same caring attention you give to your partner.

Facing Feelings, Facing Defenses

Often in the course of a session someone discovers that she has angry feelings towards her mother, father, lover, husband, child or friend. It must be pointed out that these are not the *only* feelings she has towards them, but that they *are* strong feelings in conflict with other feelings and, unless they are acknowledged by the person, they will come out in indirect ways, such as compulsive eating. If the woman tries to hide the "negative" feelings from herself, they will interfere with the relationship in confusing and destructive ways that she will neither understand nor control. (The two exercises on pages 141–144 on expressing and exploring feelings are useful for dealing with this dilemma.) ❧

It is important to remember that we all have a right to our own feelings, whatever they are (and they change). How we understand and act on them depends on our accepting the feelings in the first place. We have all become used to ignoring our feelings, either by stuffing them down before they have a chance to fully emerge or by transforming them into something else (for example, feeling miserable about being fat rather than exploring the miserable feelings in the first place). We may feel somewhat scared of experiencing them now, and may unintentionally use many different props to protect ourselves from them.

These defenses are so much a part of each person's psychological make-up that when we encounter them, we must be extremely sensitive. *Trying to bash down a defense only makes it more resilient*. This is important to remember, both in terms of how we relate to our own feelings and how we relate to others. In a group situation it may often be very easy to tell that someone is being defensive—that they seem to be erecting a wall around some inner piece of themselves. You may feel tempted to try to break the wall down, but if the person resists, respect their right to do so. We do this for good reasons. Defenses develop because we have not felt understood.

How Defenses Evolve

During early childhood all of us at one time or another have had the experience of feeling misunderstood, rejected, ridiculed or dismissed. I'm not referring to major traumatic events, but to the complex texture of ordinary communication in which our needs, desires and our feelings as children are sometimes misinterpreted by those on whom we depend. In fact, the most painful experiences can arise from surprisingly minor, everyday conversations and events that are not "outstanding" enough to be impressed on our conscious minds. The response we get leads to our feeling ashamed of these needs, desires and feelings, so we unconsciously lock them away deep inside us. We then develop defenses to protect ourselves against anticipated future hurts.

By being hidden away, our feelings are in a sense protected from dismissal or belittlement by others, but they are also not easy for us to re-examine and re-experience, and they can remain distorted and confused. Here is an example.

Mara moved from York, in the north of England, to London when she was seven years old. At her eighth birthday party she was looking a bit miserable, and her father asked warmly what was wrong. She replied, "I miss my friends from York." Her father said, "Don't be silly, dear. You have lots of lovely new friends here today."

This interaction, which on the surface was quite unremarkable, actually cut Mara to the quick. She walked away from the encounter feeling confused, terribly hurt and dreadfully ashamed. Her feeling of being miserable had not been acknowledged and thereby validated; instead, it was dismissed. Her father had indicated to her (out of his own desire to cheer her up and take away her bad feelings) that she had no reason to feel sad. Inside her, this transaction translated as follows:

1. Mara is feeling upset.
2. She is asked why.
3. She reveals her vulnerability.
4. She hears father telling her not to feel that way.
5. She feels angry at her father for not understanding her.
6. She feels nervous about her anger towards her father.
7. She feels ashamed about wanting to have been understood.
8. She wonders whether she isn't silly, wrong, to have strong feelings of missing people.
9. She sees that these feelings are not acceptable, so she knows she had better not show them again.
10. She buries them.

Hidden away and so often accompanied by shame, the feelings in a distorted form continue to affect Mara. Other incidents like this contribute to Mara's psychological development. They are like terrible sores that are re-infected because of something someone says or because current emotional pictures reproduce the past.

For instance, Mara grows up feeling that both her sad feelings and her feelings of wanting to be understood are wrong. So, in the course of growing up, she develops defenses that keep this part of her hidden. While it is hidden away from the world, it is also hidden from herself.

Once she joins a group or works on her problem herself, Mara's dilemma needs to be recognized.

Her dilemma is that she would like to get beneath her defenses but does not know how. If this can be acknowledged, then Mara will be able to feel the kind of safety that will allow her to peek beneath the defense and feel the feelings. A helpful intervention when observing defensiveness in another person might be to share with them that you have noticed their nervousness about looking into their feelings. Often by acknowledging your understanding of their fear and their need to be protective of themselves, you can create a comfortable space for them to relax such a tight grip. Bear in mind that your own defenses, and the defenses of others, are not intentional; they will best dissolve when you feel sufficient empathy to work them through.

Fat itself can be a defense. We use fatness in a protective way and an important step in coming to terms with our body image and compulsive-eating problem depends on being able to make a shift in how we relate to the fat. You are trying to develop an understanding and a relationship to it, rather than attacking yourself for being fat. In other words, *get to know your fat; don't distance yourself from it; don't pretend it isn't you.*

Your fat is a part of you; it is there (or has been) for good reason. Beating up on yourself about it doesn't give you a new solution. Try to accept it. The more you understand about your fat and the more you can accept how it expresses aspects of you, the more of its meaning you can integrate into yourself. In turn, this integration opens up the way for you to give up your need for the fat. Once the parts of you that it was protecting or representing don't have to be compartmentalized, but can be owned, you can then let go of the fat as a defense.

Group Work

The work that goes on within established compulsive-eaters groups set up along the lines discussed in *Fat Is A Feminist Issue* is also extremely relevant to women working on the problem alone or with a friend. The types of issues that come up, the ways that can be tackled and the need for self-acceptance are common to all compulsive eaters. Looking at one self-help group in action could give you greater insights into your own eating patterns and problems with body image, regardless of whether or not you are a member of a group.

The group we are going to look at has been meeting for six months at the point we've chosen to observe a session. There are six women in the group:

PAMELA is thirty-two, a school teacher, married, feels herself to be twenty pounds overweight.

JENNIFER is thirty-four, married, has an eight-year-old daughter, does knitting design. Sees herself as about thirty pounds overweight.

BELINDA is twenty-six, an architect. Not overweight, but compulsive about food.

JUDY is forty-eight, a music teacher, divorced with two children who have left home. Sees herself as slightly overweight.

KATHY is thirty-one, has one child, is living with partner, not working outside home at present, was a nurse, feels ten pounds overweight.

CAROL is forty-three, married, a housewife, has three children, twenty-one, nineteen and sixteen. Writes poetry in her spare time. Sees herself as thirty-five pounds overweight.

Of the six women, Judy has been in individual psychotherapy and Kathy has worked in psychiatric nursing. There are no other group members with a therapy background. Jennifer is the first to take her turn at this meeting.

JENNIFER: Well, I think I'd like to talk about this weekend when I went home to visit my parents and I had a really difficult time with food—as per usual. And I would really like Pamela to listen especially carefully and help me out if necessary. Is that okay with everyone?

PAMELA: It's fine with me.

GROUP: Sounds okay. I'm sure we will all be able to identify with what it's like to go home.

JENNIFER: Isn't it strange that we call it home, even when in my case I've had my own home for fifteen years. Anyway, I'd decided to visit my parents. Bob couldn't come, so I went for the day with Rachel [*her daughter*], as I thought she would enjoy being able to run around helping my parents around the garden.

So we arrived about 11:30 a.m., and Rachel and my father went into the garden. My mother was waiting for us, but didn't, as per usual, express any real enthusiasm about seeing either of us. She just sort of sat there in the way I've described before, waiting for me to make all the effort, entertain her, tell her things she could talk to her friends about, and never asking me anything real, and so on. At least now I can feel my fury mounting inside of me over the whole set-up.

Anyway, I just had to hold it all in and remind myself that I was only there for a few hours. But, of course, that didn't exactly work because [*cries and is clenching her fists*] when it came time to sit down for lunch, I knew I was going to overeat and I did. I didn't eat exactly compulsively, but I did feel that I ate more than I wanted and that I got up from the table feeling physically uncomfortable. Then when I was clearing off the table and doing the dishes, I just sort of scoffed the leftovers—I mean, can you imagine—the leftovers in my mother's house—[*Cries.*]—Oh, I feel so frustrated and angry—[*Silence for about three minutes, then Jennifer looks over at Pam.*]

PAMELA: Would it help to try and go through some of those heavy emotions with a bit of breathing space here?

JENNIFER: Yeah, but I don't know how to.

PAMELA: Well, I noticed that you said you had to hold your fury and upset; perhaps you could try to feel it here now in the group—

JENNIFER: I don't know what to do to feel it.

PAMELA: Well, let's focus on what you were feeling when you were on your way to your mother's.

JENNIFER: Well, as usual when I made the plan, it was done out of guilt, not to disappoint her, done because I feel Rachel's entitled to have grandparents. So I suppose I felt at first I was doing my duty. Then on the way out there, I got my usual pangs of wanting it to be nice—which is so stupid of me. I'm really wrong for wanting something from her. So, of course I'm sure I arrived in a state of wanting—I know I did. Rachel ran out of the car to greet my parents; they kissed me lightly on the cheek. I suppose I felt a bit ignored. [*Sighs.*] I definitely felt ignored, passed over, not seen. [*Weeps.*] Oh, God. I feel so overwhelmed with that feeling now, but guess what I did. It's so uncanny. Automatically I found myself in the refrigerator—searching for God knows what. [*Laughs.*] Oh, to enter that house without having to open that fridge door—it's so bare anyway; nothing nice in it. [*Sits quietly for about three minutes.*] I feel that day is such a microcosm of my problem. I don't feel seen as myself; I feel my mom taking things from me, and then it's like I stealthily take from her.

PAMELA: Does it help clarify anything to look at the act of overeating in terms of the message you might be asking your "fat" to convey to her?

JENNIFER: Yes, you're right. I feel she can't ignore me. She hates fat, my mother does, being a dieter all her life, so she'll—or rather I think I'm trying to say to her, "Hey, you don't ignore me—look at me, see—" Also, I'm somewhat desperate and I think it's maybe a way to show her how angry I am. [*Sits quietly.*] If I feel it in terms of the emotions my overeating is expressing, I'd say anger over not being given to. [*Cries and bangs on the floor with her right foot.*] I feel I've got to allow these emotions to come up a bit more as they have been recently and not convert them into silent, aggressive fat—

Thanks, I feel I've had enough time.

PAMELA: Are you sure?

JENNIFER: Yes.

KATHY: Can I ask something, Jennifer?

JENNIFER: Sure.

KATHY: Well, something occurred to me when you were talking when you first described going to your mom's. You said you were stupid for still wanting things from her, and I heard you being *so* self-punishing with yourself. I do that to myself all the time. I want something from my mother, and she can't give it and then I blame myself for wanting. Somehow, hearing you say it clarified something for me, and I wondered if we all take out on ourselves others' inadequacies. I mean, it's not your fault your mother is a bit cold, nor that mine is overbearing, and yet we both think it is.

JENNIFER: If only I could feel that.

TIMEKEEPER: It's getting close to the end of your time. What would you like to do now?

JENNIFER: Does anyone else know what I'm on about it?

GROUP: Absolutely.

JENNIFER: It's such a relief to know I'm not totally isolated in these kinds of dilemmas. Thanks for all your attention; I really appreciate it.

TIMEKEEPER: Before we move on to the next person, perhaps we should each take a minute to think quietly to ourselves about how we were all affected by the things Jennifer experienced.

This gives group members a chance to be in contact with whatever feelings were triggered off for them. This minimizes the chance that people will then ask questions out of their own needs, rather than in the explicit interest of the member who is presenting her problem. The more the group can design intervals for silent reflection, to allow each member to see what is going on inside herself, the easier it will be to minimize the difficulties that can arise over misidentification.

Jennifer's story about her visit with her mother stirred up, in other group members, similar feelings of disappointment, wanting and anger towards their families. Some members felt temporarily confused about what they wanted to work on in their time that session. Giving members a chance to reflect on their own experiences provides a certain breathing space in which each can see what is most important for her to discuss that night. It may be what each one had in mind originally, or it may be something akin to Jennifer's experience.

TIMEKEEPER: Okay, who would like to talk next?

JUDY: Well, I've got something on my mind. I've really noticed that for the last month or so, since my weight has been lower and I'm looking closer to what I really want—in fact I'm at my imagined slim size—I take almost every opportunity to just slightly overeat. It's almost as though I can't just accept my success. I'm defeating myself or playing games with myself. It's so upsetting, because in one way I feel I have really understood so much and put it into practice, and here I'm almost deliberately sabotaging myself.

BELINDA: Are you scared of being your ideal size?

PAMELA: Do you think you could be worried about being slim?

JUDY: Hang on—one at a time.

It is important in the group to agree that the person whose time it is has as much say over what happens in that time as possible. So, for example, if group members ask a lot of questions simultaneously, or fire off too many questions so that it makes it hard to assimilate them and use them usefully, the person who is on can and should say, "Back off" or "Stop" or "No more questions please." She should feel free to direct others' interventions in ways that make more sense and are truly helpful to her.

JUDY: What did you ask, Belinda?

BELINDA: I was wondering whether you were worried about having actually achieved your ideal size.

JUDY: Well, I must be because I seem to be quite preoccupied with the whole thing. It really does feel almost deliberate and a bit self-destructive, like I'm not allowed to enjoy what's going on for me.

PAMELA: Suppose you were your ideal size and it wasn't a precarious state of affairs—

JUDY: I can't really feel that. Maybe if I just think of being more relaxed around food. I think I get scared that I won't know what to do with all that time I spend preoccupied with food and weight—Sometimes I realize I haven't been that obsessed for a day or so, but I have felt a bit anxious and I don't know why—a sort of general anxiety and fragility. I can feel it now, just talking about it, and I feel like shuddering away from. There obviously is some major reason why I'm scared to be slim. [*Looks scared.*] Partly it feels like it has to do with envy and not having a place—My younger sister was always slim and very pretty, and I feel she gets so much attention from everyone in the family. Everybody sort of clucks over her and I suppose I've always felt outside of the competition, like I wasn't— [*Cries.*] I feel I'm not good enough and that she gets it all and I've always had an excuse for that for myself. I've been that fat, reliable, older sister who stood in for Mom—I think I'm really scared of renouncing that role and asking to be seen in another way. It makes me feel all queasy inside.

BELINDA: In a way, that sounds really good, like you are having the feelings you often run away from.

JUDY: But it is scary to think of competing with my sister, or even just changing my self-image and not being the dependable one in the background. I mean, that is so much a part of the way I've seen myself— I want to change. I want to bring other parts of me forward, although I do feel a bit ashamed of the attention-seeking me. But I know I have to try because the queasy feelings won't go away unless I do—I feel I've sort of cheated myself for a long time. I'm not sure what is at the other side of the attention, but I think I want to find out. You know, I think behind my fat was a very energetic me trying to get out........
.... (sits quietly reflecting) ....

Would someone please come to my house and help me fling out my clothes, or at least sort them out? I might be too scared to part with them immediately. I feel most of the things I wear don't really express who I feel I am; they are so dowdy.

GROUP: Maybe we could go shopping with you. You wouldn't necessarily have to buy, but you could try on various styles and experiment.

JUDY: That would be great. Who could come to my house on Tuesday or Thursday?

PAMELA: I can come tomorrow.

JUDY: Great.

TIMEKEEPER: Do you want to arrange a shopping trip, too?

JUDY: I think I need to do the cleaning out first. Maybe next week I could take some of my time to report in on that experience and then see whether I would like some help trying out new styles. At any rate, I feel I've had enough time for today.

TIMEKEEPER: Does anyone identify with Judy? Think about what might have been set off in you when she was talking. Let's sit for a minute and think about it.

KATHY: I really identify with the part about feeling frumpish, but for me it's more to do with my mother. Shall I go on? I could use my time to work on it.

CAROL: Well, I identify, too, but differently because my sister was the one with the "brains" and I was the pretty one with the personality. It's so ridiculous because we both suffered from being seen that way. She never felt really adequate, and was always scared of talking, and I've never really felt okay in my body—but why don't you talk now, Kathy?

KATHY: Well, you know how I've said my mother always takes such incredible care of herself. If she wasn't my mother, I think I'd think she was horribly vain, but because she is my mother, I feel, or at any rate I've always felt, thoroughly infuriated by her bottles of perfume, creams, lipsticks, her dresses and shoes. I can remember so well when I was little watching her getting ready to go out. She'd be wrapped in a sort of magic aura—queenlike to me—it was lovely. But I suppose although all of that was so close, it was also not for me in some profound way. And I think in some very private place I've thought of it as a vanity that is allowed to beautiful women, but not to plain ones like me. So it's sort of okay that she primped herself, but it would be obscene if I did.

CAROL: But why do you think you are plain? You are anything but dowdy, although it is true you don't project all that you could. I think you are really attractive. You've got a really nice body, and you are very attractive. You've always seemed so nonchalant to me about it. In fact, I've thought of you as someone who sort of took the fact of their being good-looking for granted and was at ease with it all.

KATHY: But I don't feel that way at all. I feel awkward and not very clear how I look or how I'd like to look, and sort of ashamed of being interested in the whole topic in the first place. Recently I've been looking in magazines and at people on the street and wondering how they put their images together and being almost intrigued like a little girl at a magic show.

PAMELA: But isn't that the thing we were all talking about a few sessions ago when we were saying we were never shown how to be women? We felt no one, especially not our mothers, had helped us learn how to dress or appreciate our bodies.

KATHY: It's true, and it seems to go so deep. I even feel that, beyond not getting help from my mother, I was even discouraged from seeing my feminine side, if you know what I mean. I remember all the no's and don't's about being a girl, but I can't remember any of the things I imagine other girls had—touching, shopping, talking about appearance. Maybe nobody did get it, but I feel anyway as a result that part of me feels very inadequate at all the feminine stuff and a bit ashamed of being inadequate.

JENNIFER: This might not be the right thing to say just now, but I was wondering if you couldn't use the group to get just that kind of attention—I mean, we all think you are lovely, obviously, and we understand that you can't exactly feel that, but I'd be very happy to help sort through things about image and femininity here.

KATHY: I feel I've got such an awful self-image really, and I even feel talking here that I don't know if you do all feel that accepting, but I know that is *my* problem, and yes I would like to do more about it.

PAMELA: Well, maybe you could do something now that might help, which would be to think of one of those images you noticed and liked and then try to put it on yourself. Do you understand?

KATHY: Feels a bit phony, taking something that isn't me and putting it on—

PAMELA: Well, it is. But it's more like trying things out that you might have wanted to try before but haven't felt it's okay to do. I agree it isn't integrated, but it is a start.

KATHY: Well, if I can get past all the rubbish, there is a look I go for. I suppose it's what's describable as sort of a sixties' look—I don't know—sort of elegant bohemian, a bit like how you dress, Belinda. Nice lines—but I suppose you know how to do that, because you have a good sense of design. If I could dress like that, I might project myself better.

JENNIFER: Well, why don't you imagine you are dressed like that—head to toe, you know—bag, jewelry, the whole thing—and just see what happens.

[*A big smile comes over Kathy's face.*]

In this interaction, the group is in effect providing the looking after, and giving Kathy the permission she feels she's never had from adult women to explore and express what she would like to do with her body.

[*Kathy straightens her body, changes her seating position and sees how that feels.*]

BELINDA: We're near enough the same size. Would you like to try some of my things on?

KATHY: Well, I've always wanted to wear a shirt and jacket like you do.

BELINDA: Here. [*She takes them off.*] Try them on.

[*Kathy puts them on but resumes her old posture.*]

JENNIFER: Now, why don't you try sitting or standing in a way that goes with that look for you?

KATHY: It feels really nice. Can I go look in the mirror? [*She goes to the mirror.*] Well, now I know what feels so hard about all this. I look a lot like my aunt, my dad's sister, who was sort of described as a tough woman but with a bit of a wink. I always got the impression that my mother didn't approve of her because she was single and had lovers and was risqué in her day. It's hard to hold myself this way, because I'm so habituated to looking frumpish, but this does feel a bit more like the me I wouldn't mind being.

BELINDA: When you started to talk, you said you didn't really feel you knew what you would like to project, but maybe you do. It doesn't seem all so elusive—or maybe you want to experiment more with other looks?

KATHY: What feels important out of this is it just being okay to even think about these things.

BELINDA: Maybe we should spend a whole session discussing this. I'd like to bring in clothes to try on that I feel I can't wear out of the house, although I bought them. I feel I could get some accurate feedback here about whether I look ridiculous in them.

GROUP MEMBERS: I think that's a good idea, because we all seem so confused by this stuff.

CAROL: I don't even know what images I like—that's how cut off I am! I think it will be great.

PAMELA: Maybe we could also think of it in terms of women in our family and how their images affect us.

This is an aspect of self-image you may want to explore on your own. Consider how all the women in your family may have affected your image of yourself. Were they fat or thin? What was each one's role within the family group—was she admired, loved, feared, hated, resented, exploited, crushed, ostracized, imitated? Explore the unspoken judgments that rush into your mind if you see yourself looking a certain way. Whom do you remind yourself of? Allow yourself time to notice what feelings come up for you, and try giving yourself permission to have the feelings and still dress that way.

As this session continued, Pamela discussed an aspect of body image that was important for her—dislike of her large breasts. She discussed how she has never really enjoyed her body because of them and that she stays away from slimness because she doesn't have a perfect body. This way, she doesn't have to cope with that fact. If she were slim, she thinks, she would feel just as dissatisfied with her body and her breasts would seem proportionately bigger. She's scared of getting pregnant because her breasts would be so large that she'd look like only breasts and stomach.

Other members of the group responded in several ways. First, they pointed out that she had a distorted view of her body—when she looked in the mirror, she only saw breasts, but when they looked at her, they saw a whole body. They also pointed out that she was usually hunched over, which emphasized rather than hid her breasts. They also commented that, as her size had been gradually changing since she'd joined the group, so too had her breasts. They hadn't stayed exactly the same, but had decreased in proportion. Pamela began to focus her attention on the feelings of loathing she had towards her body—when they began and what was beneath them.

Belinda talked about how she was beginning to realize that she was fearful of success, both in terms of her work as an architect and in accepting her body and her looks. She noticed that she undermined herself constantly without even knowing it until the end of the day when she reviewed her food intake and noticed the many self-defeating ways in which she had acted. It emerged that she was frightened of the independence her work success was enabling her to achieve and having difficulty accepting the gulf she felt it opened up between her and other people. She found this feeling most unsettling.

The group worked with her to see where her compulsive eating fit into this, and she thought that it might be that the compulsive eating was a way in which she was blurring the edges and expressing her fear of being defined. She also thought that she might be focusing on her food as a way to avoid confronting the much harder conflict that was emerging for her around work.

Carol talked about how upset she felt about her sexuality and her relationship with her husband. She felt her fat was keeping her in the marriage, and that she couldn't afford to lose weight because then she would have to face how much she desired the sexual and emotional contact that she felt was lacking in the marriage. She didn't feel her marriage could improve in the ways she would like, but at the same time, she was scared of separation. Since joining the group, she had been very attracted to another man, and they had discussed having a love affair. But she felt she couldn't be unfaithful to her husband. She was afraid that if she could attract and be attracted to a man at her current size, it meant her sexuality was almost uncontrollable and could create more serious problems if she were slimmer. In the group, she tried to begin to sort through the confusions about sexuality, size, attraction. There was no resolution, but she came away thinking about how strongly sexual she felt and how she might express it.

In this particular session, then, themes emerged that are extremely common in women with compulsive-eating problems. In each case, the women were not able to feel comfortable around food or in their bodies. Each woman had fantasies about who she might be (different from who she currently was), if she were to feel or project slimness.

For Carol, slimness was linked with sexuality; for Belinda, slimness meant being separate and independent; for Pamela, slimness meant she would have to accept herself—as long as she wasn't slim, she could blame her imperfections on her fatness; for Kathy, slimness meant allowing herself to look somewhat dashing; for Judy, slimness meant getting attention in a different, unfamiliar way; for Jennifer, slimness stirred up worries that she wouldn't be seen.

These concerns are intertwined with unconscious fantasies about the symbolic meanings of fatness and what fat is expressing for the individual woman. After more than six months of meeting as a group, these women all gained sufficient understanding of their inner processes to realize slimness had eluded them for "good reason," that they weren't just lacking in self-control and will-power but that their compulsive eating was a reactive and protective mechanism that they employed when they could not cope with underlying conflicts in a more direct way.

How to Ask Questions

If we review this session, we can see that, by sticking to very simple questions and being disciplined about leaving time for those questions to filter through to the member they were directed at, individuals in the group can "work" effectively at a psychological level together. It is expecially important to be careful, as this group was, not to plunge in or bombard each other with queries. Help each other pursue the feelings that are behind the compulsive eating and the symbolic meaning of fat and thin for each of you.

When you ask questions of each other, be sure to leave time for the answer to stir up something inside rather than to provoke a quick intellectual reply. Don't push hard on the questions; that isn't the point. Offer them and if they aren't useful, think again and see if you can get inside the other person's shoes momentarily to see what they might be experiencing.

There are an almost infinite number of questions that might be helpful. The point isn't to show how well one can ask questions, but to do so in a way that both strikes a core issue and gives the other person the chance to respond. For example, the possible questions that might have been useful to Jennifer (the first woman who spoke in the group session just described) to help her break her automatic walk to the refrigerator in her mother's house include the following:

1. Can you say what you were looking for?
2. What are you looking to find out?
3. How old do you feel at the refrigerator door?
4. What would you like to find when you open the refrigerator door?
5. What are the feelings you are rushing to cover up by eating?
6. What would happen if you didn't go straight to the fridge?

Another possible intervention would have been to focus on any aspect of the day that Jennifer had described, linking it to her longings, her feeling of not being noticed, her desire to "over" eat and her wish to get something from her mother. For example, Jennifer might have found it helpful to talk about the meal itself, in which case the following line of questioning could have been useful to her:

1. Do you know what you were feeling when you sat down at the table?
2. What was your mother serving?
3. Did the food have any particular meaning for you?
4. What were mealtimes like for you when you lived at home?
5. What was the atmosphere at the table?
6. Did you play a particular role at the table?
7. Do you know what you were feeling at the precise moment when you crossed the line from eating comfortably to eating more than you wanted?

When asking questions, it is important to bear in mind several points:

1. Ask questions one by one, leaving plenty of time for the person to digest each question and respond to it (or reject it as unhelpful).
2. Ask questions from a perspective that is sympathetic to each woman's dilemma. Try to think about where she is stuck and then ask your question with the intention of helping to open up the stuck area.
3. Ask questions which elicit feelings, not concepts or impersonal abstractions. The point is not to satisfy your curiosity or clear up your own confusion.
4. If you aren't sure why you want to ask any particular question, ask it of yourself first. It may have more to do with you. Then reconsider whether it would be helpful to the other person.

5. Remember that you offer a question as an aid to the other person. Try not to feel rejected if she doesn't find it useful.

It is *not* useful or appropriate to tell the speaker if you find yourself feeling bored while she is working. This is much more likely to be a clue to what is happening for *you* than for her. Look inside yourself to check whether you might be withdrawing your attention in order to stop your own painful or unpleasant feelings from coming up, or if the boredom could be part of an unresolved conflict that already exists between you and the speaker.

Difficulties around food are often particularly noticeable in ❀ family situations. Childhood experiences of eating with parents can be very important in understanding present-day compulsive-eating patterns, even if these now occur in many other settings as well as at home. To explore the links between your own early food history and your current eating behavior, turn to the exercise "The Family Meal," on page 157.

Replaying Difficult Times

Another type of intervention that might have been useful to ❀ Jennifer would have been to suggest that she reenact the scene at her parents' house, but this time to see if she could *not* overeat at lunch, and instead allow those feelings that she was stuffing down through food to rise to the surface. (The exercise "Increasing Your Food Awareness," which you'll find on page 137 could be helpful for this.)

Jennifer would thus remember back to the meal itself and all her associated feelings. She would allow the scene to play through her mind briefly, focusing in on the point when she continued to eat even though she wasn't physically hungry. Stopping at this point, Jennifer would try to feel what had been going on inside her. She might notice feelings of anger towards her mother. She might feel very troubled by such feelings, and rather scared of them.

A good way for Jennifer to explore and discharge such angry feelings would be to ask one of the other group members to play act being Jennifer's mother so that Jennifer could tell her mother what angered and upset her. By doing this, she might be able to get the feelings off her chest in a safe place without fearing her mother's real reaction, and she might discover that her feelings were in fact less overwhelming than she had imagined. Through this preparatory method Jennifer could see what it was like to acknowledge that she did indeed have angry feelings towards her mother. She could then decide what to do about them in reality. (The exercise on expressing feelings, on page 141, could also be useful for this.)

Ending a Group Meeting

After the last person in a group has finished speaking, it is a good idea to allow fifteen minutes or so for the group to discuss what you might like to do at your next session. This might mean selecting an exercise together and having the timekeeper for the next week's meeting take responsibility for bringing a prerecorded tape of the chosen exercise.

Then, to end the meeting, the current week's timekeeper could ask all the group members to sit quietly for a minute or two to think about what each of them would be taking away from the session. This time to refocus attention on yourself also allows an opportunity for anyone who may be in particular emotional discomfort and may feel loath to leave the group, or may feel the need to get something off her chest, to have her need acknowledged before she leaves. So, at the very end of the session, you may decide to build in the option for people to say how they are feeling.

Here is what the members voiced at the end of the meeting we've been observing:

PAMELA: I feel so much better now, although I certainly do have a lot to think about. Thanks so much all of you for being so understanding and helpful.

BELINDA: I feel a bit nervous with what I talked about, like the insight could just slip away or I could bury it under eating, so I could use some checking in with so that I don't.

GROUP: Well, we could check in with you next session but in the meantime maybe you should have a homework assignment to write down what feelings you are trying to stuff down instead of eating them away, and see how difficult it is to actually hold on to them.

BELINDA: Thanks, that's a good idea, I'll try it.

CAROL: I feel so relieved to have talked about what I did but I also feel HELP! I'm scared!

GROUP: That is so understandable and also you must remember that you don't have to act on anything, you are just trying to sort things out for the present and you can fantasize leaving your husband or having affairs without doing anything until you feel comfortable.

JUDY: Well, I feel a lot better just saying what I did tonight.

KATHY: Me too and I'm always amazed about where this subject takes me. I start off on one thing and end up with such a bigger and more intense view of things.

JENNIFER: I know what you mean. I always feel worse and better at the end of a session. You know I'm determined to go to my mother's one day and not overeat!

Spending a Day Together

A day spent with other compulsive eaters can give you a chance to inject new energy into the work you're doing. You can do a variety of exercises together that will not only give you data to explore later, it will also give a group a cohesive feeling after having interacted together in a different way. If you would like to spend a day together, I suggest you make arrangements to be in a large, comfortable room, and to make sure that you won't be disturbed. Plan some of the day in advance and keep some of it open so that spontaneous happenings don't necessarily have to be nipped in the bud. If you feel you want to relax the equal-time rule that operates in most groups, do put in its place a carefully thought-out exercise or topic that makes sense for each person to concentrate on and which takes into account the different needs of each woman.

The compulsive-eating group of six women that was described in the previous sections decided to meet from 10 a.m. to 6 p.m. on a Saturday. They agreed in advance that they would also use the time together to try eating when they were hungry and stopping when they were satisfied. To help this work, they decided to bring along a variety of foods that they knew they liked to eat.

Each woman was to eat when she felt hungry. They did not make planned breaks for food, although there was a break in the middle of the day to talk conversationally, stretch, take a walk or, of course, eat if anyone was hungry. Each woman was to take responsibility for mentioning to the group when she had a desire to eat and was not physically hungry, or when she had a desire to continue eating past the point of having satisfied her stomach hunger. In this way, she could do an on-the-spot investigation of what was motivating her compulsive eating at that time.

Choosing Exercises: Dress as Your Mother

With these minimum guidelines set, the group chose the following activities for the day. Kathy very much wanted to work on creating a self-image that felt right for her. She proposed an exercise that would go to the heart of what she thought was her problem: the confusion between her identity as a woman and the overwhelming picture of her mother's femininity. She thought that if she could try acting as her mother, she might be able to get the physical presence of her out of her system and in that way come to grips with her own physicalness. She suggested coming to the group dressed as her mother and seeing where that took her.

The other women were so taken by her idea that each decided to dress up as her own mother. As it turned out, the awkwardness, excitement and the different aspects of each personality that became emphasized made for a very energetic opening to the day. The women were all involved in a rather exposing activity together and were able to handle their complicated feelings about emulating their mothers directly and with warmth. Nearly everyone was shocked to realize how much like her mother she felt herself to be. This led to a major discussion about the role of their mothers in their conceptions of self.

In acting their mothers, this group of women found out where some of their internal judging voices came from. For nearly all the group members, it was a revelation to discover that they looked at themselves with what felt like their mother's eyes. During the course of the exercise, they "role-played," talking to their mothers about their figures and their food. The despair, judgments and hopes that their mothers seemed to have pinned on them were almost mirror reflections of their own views.

In realizing how much of their picture of their mothers lived inside of each of them, the way was open to look into not so much the why of it all, but into what to do about it. Kathy, for instance, felt that her attachment to her mother in this way acted as a barrier to her being her own person. Once she had experienced that realization in a very stark way, she needed to come to grips with not hiding herself behind her internal mother.

Jennifer realized that much of her strong feeling of wanting from her mother was an echo of the longing she felt her mother had wordlessly expressed to *her* throughout her childhood. She realized that the terribly disappointed feelings she always experienced around her mother and the bitterness that accompanied those feelings were similar to the attitude she experienced as emanating from her mother. Jennifer felt the weight of her mother's unsatisfied emotional life and saw that she was headed down the same path unless she actively intervened. She realized that, for her mother, nothing was ever good enough and that her mother often acted as though she were bound to get the raw end of any deal. Dressing up as her mother was a startling confrontation for Jennifer. She realized that the very aspects of her mother that distressed her were, in fact, a large part of how she experienced herself.

Pamela felt that this exercise provided her with a new experience regarding her breasts. Dressing and holding herself as her mother, she realized that she felt her body to be very similar to her mother's— *except* for her large breasts. She remembered how ashamed she had felt when she first wanted a bra and there was nobody with whom she could talk about it. She had felt she couldn't turn to her mother, because her mother had still seen her as a little girl.

The re-experiencing of this incident, which she had thought about many times but had never really *felt*, released Pamela in some very important way. She described it as feeling the blood flow back into her chest. She tried to hold her back straight and really felt for the first time just how hunched over she was and how that had been a response to feeling uncomfortable with her developing breasts. Because she had been holding herself that way for so long, she decided to find out about exercises that would help her straighten up.

In this exercise, each woman was able to identify a part of herself with a part of how she saw her mother. This can be a very powerful experience as our ingrained habits of internal condemnation are shown for what they are—thereby becoming less automatic and inhibiting.

The Chinese Meal Exercise

Another exercise this group did focused on food. In it they imagined a birthday party for themselves at a Chinese restaurant. This exercise is aimed at opening up the following questions:

1. How do you feel about sharing your special day with others around food?
2. Who orders the food?
3. Does each guest, or does the birthday person or her partner do it?
4. Are you able to invite only the people you really want?
5. What are the conflicts, if any, at the table.
6. If there are any, how are they played out through the food?

If you would like to do this exercise for yourself, turn to page 161.
When this group did the exercise, all the women felt really good about having a meal for their birthday. As far as food ordering was concerned, three of them wanted the food to be a surprise and the others felt very strongly that they wanted to be sure of having their favorite dishes. Everyone felt they couldn't really invite only whom they wanted to their party; in each case there was an unwanted guest whom the birthday person felt she couldn't offend by not inviting. This realization was quite important, because it expressed at a level other than food and fat the issue of feeling it was impossible to define or show themselves as they felt they were inside.

When each woman asked herself how coming up with a guest list that was absolutely right for her could affect how she felt at the party and in relation to the food, this seemed to raise a feeling that things would be "too good." They felt, in varying degrees, a certain anxiety if life turned out just as they wanted—either it was impossible or they didn't deserve it.

These responses, which at first glance may seem surprising, stem from our experiences of growing up female. If we are encouraged to devote our energies, concerns and hopes to others—especially our families—we may experience an internal confusion, a wrench, once we begin to turn that attention towards ourselves and try to pursue what *we* would like. This kind of anxiety, which may be expressing a fear of "getting too much," is a reaction that many women experience in the process of trying to be more self-determining. It is something you are quite likely to feel if you are trying to change the habit of repressing your own needs.

Body Image Exercises

Another exercise this group did focused on body image. They imagined that they were all as fat as they had ever feared, and they acted out being at a party and circulating with the other guests. They walked around the room and talked with each other, feeling how it was to be in that situation. Then they changed their posture and walked around, talking to each other as though they were all slim and their ideal size.

What is striking is the difference each time you do this exercise. You may be able to feel that a part of you is resisting slimness and, at the same time, be aware of the pain that goes along with being fat and feeling excluded and different. For most women, the pain is a definite step forward from the blind self-hatred that once accompanied any recognition of their fat selves.

You can also re-use the fat/thin fantasy exercise on page 145 as often as you like, either on your own or in a group. It too will help you to experience whatever emotions are connected with fatness and thinness for you.

Often, like Pamela, we tend to focus our feelings of dislike for our bodies on to one particular body part. We can, as a result, develop a rather distorted view of that part. It can leap out at you whenever you look in the mirror and seem much more prominent than it really is. You may imagine that your problems would be solved *if only* your breasts/thighs/hips/legs/tummy weren't so . . . Similarly, you may fantasize that the shape of that part will change completely when you reach your ideal size. Regardless of whether this is always the same area of your body or a succession of different ones, such dissecting always leads to judging, which gets in the way of self-acceptance.

The "Part of the Body" exercise can help you to explore the meaning of your distress about various body parts and to work through the barriers to feeling at ease in your body. The feelings we have about our bodies and various aspects of our bodies are constantly changing. By using the exercise from time to time, you will be able to experience that movement for yourself. After you do the "Part of the Body" exercise, which is on page 153, refer to the questions below.

1. What kind of associations did you come up with to this part of your body?
2. Do any other members of your family share the same concern about this part of their body?
3. If so, how do you feel about that part of their body?
4. Now spend some time exploring the themes that came up for you when you were doing the fantasy. Think through in detail your first awareness of your discomfort with this part of your body. What kind of role does this discomfort play currently, and what are the emotional issues this discomfort is masking? Are you perhaps assigning it more power than it has? Does being preoccupied with this part *help* you in any way?
5. Why do you so dislike this part? Is it because it doesn't conform to a stereotype? If in the fantasy you superimposed someone else's body part on to yours, whose was it—and what does that mean for you? If you saw yourself younger, what was so special about that particular time?
6. What is the actual bodily function of this part of your body? How well does it perform its physical function? How do you feel about its function?

Looking at Feelings

Another exercise this group did focused on whatever emotion each of them was having difficulty with at the time. In this they were touching on important issues that compulsive eaters have to grapple with because, as we have seen, so often compulsive eating serves to cover up or transform feelings. Carol, for instance, wanted a chance to look at her angry feelings—what was so awful about them that she felt she had to eat them away. Belinda felt she always ran away from feelings of sadness; Pamela wanted to see where her enthusiastic feelings had disappeared to; Judy and Kathy focused on their competitive feelings towards other women; Jennifer wanted to get more in touch with her guilt feelings.

This exercise was designed by Luise Eichenbaum and myself for many of the single-topic workshops, held at the Women's Therapy Centre in London, that are aimed at pinpointing key issues such as anger, jealousy, competition, giving and receiving, dependency and difficulty with power. You can do it equally well on your own at home. It gives you a chance to explore your feelings and reflect on them.

If you take your time over it, the exercise will also help you to sit with the uncomfortable feelings. This very process of giving yourself time may be a novel experience for you, because frequently compulsive eaters find that they only experience for a microsecond the feelings that cause them pain and upset. The feelings are then rapidly buried, either under an avalanche of food or because they have developed psychological mechanisms that cut them off. These inaccessible feelings often seem quite scary, but this exercise (which you can use frequently) can help you gently reacquaint yourself with your subterranean feelings. It can also provide valuable insights into why certain feelings cause you distress.

When we give ourselves the chance to explore a feeling, often we discover that another (perhaps more confusing) feeling lies behind it. This is another reason for pacing yourself so that you can catch hold of the nuances of the feelings and come to accept them. Often the reason the feeling causes so much upset is that you can't accept having the feeling, or else the feeling itself is masking another feeling that makes you even more uncomfortable.

You may want to turn to page 143 now, and try the exercise "Exploring Your Feelings."

You may find that some of your reactions to the exercise mirror those of the women in this group. Judy, a music teacher, discovered that her competitive feelings were a lot more complicated than she had at first thought. She noticed that these very painful feelings came up a lot when she thought about her musical capabilities in relation to those of her most proficient students. At first, she condemned herself for even feeling competitive in the first place, but what emerged from behind the feelings of competition were deeper feelings of regret that she hadn't taken her desire for professional recognition more seriously.

Judy realized that her competitive feelings towards others functioned to stop the pain she felt about her own life. It wasn't that the people who brought out competitive feelings in her were necessarily competitive themselves, or especially blessed, or even that they could be blamed for stirring up these feelings in her. It was rather that her focus on her competitive feelings towards them acted as a blocking mechanism that was stopping her from looking at the real issues in her life. She was projecting her own internal conflicts around ambition onto others.

Kathy's competitive feelings arose from feelings of being inadequate and excluded by others. The competitive feelings she felt towards others in this case were more an expression of her internal feelings about not accepting herself and not feeling sure that she had a right to good things out of life. The competitive feelings were almost a psychological stick that she unwittingly beat herself with, reinforcing her underlying feelings of exclusion and inadequacy. She recognized this as another aspect of her struggle to feel valid and legitimate.

Pamela noticed that her feelings of enthusiasm drained out of her when her husband didn't relate to her as she wished he would. She sometimes felt that her husband didn't understand her and what she wanted. She longed for contact but it was almost as though her emotional engagement shut off, and in its place she had to face her feelings of disappointment and frustration.

Feelings and Femininity

As we allow ourselves to explore in more depth the feelings that caused us confusion and anguish, we often notice the internal taboos that operate against our feeling whole, that keep us from being in touch with and from expressing our emotions. In other words the social restrictions that all women grow up with are reflected at the psychological level. These social practices are enforced legally, economically, politically, ideologically and culturally, through our education in our families and at school and in the ways we come to experience ourselves from the inside in our emotional lives as somehow less than, not deserving—in short, as second class.

When we as women begin to review our experience of life, we are involved in the process both of transforming our way of seeing things and of changing what we can do. Consciousness-raising is a very powerful tool for opening up new territory at all levels. The aspects of ourselves that are touched at a personal level, however, can be as painful as they are exhilarating. I have noticed time and again in my practice how shocked we all are to discover that deep inside our emotional lives we are subject to a kind of internal policing that serves to keep us in our place. This makes tremendous sense, however, because one does not grow up female without absorbing powerful lessons about who one can and cannot be.

I can't stress how important it is to *be generous to yourself* when exploring these uncomfortable emotional revelations. Often you will discover feelings inside of you that may feel divergent from the new model of yourself that you would like to be. But don't shy away from coming to grips with these feelings. They tell us an enormous amount about who we are, our personal histories, and what we need to work on in order to move forward.

Frequently, women in therapy have told me how uneasy they become when they contact their feelings of jealousy, envy or competition towards other women. They can feel so uncomfortable that they fear investigating them further, lest they uncover even more distressing things. The discovery of these complicated and sometimes disturbing feelings, however, can deepen our understanding not only of how we as individual women come to be who we are, but also of how deep are the psychological consequences of a society that denies us aspects of personhood on the basis of gender.

If we are trying to break out of the rigid sex roles in which we live, we need to have as much knowledge as possible about how they operate, both at the social and at the emotional level, so that when we try to change things we recognize the interrelationship between the personal and political world. Finding out that women carry deep feelings of inadequacy, isolation, unentitlement, inhibition, anger and rage strengthens our understanding of how the world operates and points to how seriously disabling women's oppression is.

Jennifer, for example, discovered that entwined with her guilt feelings were feelings of rebellion, bitterness and fear. She described an incident that involved her husband Bob, her daughter Rachel and the compulsive-eaters group. It was their accepted practice that Bob looked after Rachel on Tuesday evenings so that Jennifer could be free to do whatever she wanted. In fact, Tuesday came to be the night of her compulsive-eaters group, and she looked forward to getting out of the house, meeting a friend for a drink, and then going on to her meeting.

At lunchtime one Tuesday Bob was unexpectedly offered a ticket to see a play he was interested in. He wanted to go, but he did not make any alternative plans to have Rachel looked after. When he came home from work he just assumed that Jennifer would understand how important it was for him to see the play and that she would stand in for him this time. So at 6 p.m., just as Jennifer was preparing to leave the house with her friend, Bob walked in and told her about the play.

Jennifer and her friend immediately rang the other group members and asked them to meet at her house that night. After the group left later that evening, Jennifer ate compulsively and was plagued by guilt feelings. One of the women hadn't been reached in time and had arrived at the original meeting place only to have to journey again to get to Jennifer's.

Jennifer realized that she had felt distracted during the whole evening and hadn't felt able to concentrate. Partly she was listening for Rachel, hoping that she wouldn't be disturbed or disturbing. Given the fact that she had psychologically absented herself from the group session, she felt very bad about having rearranged the meeting place in such short notice.

Before Jennifer did the exercise around looking at feelings, she had been aware of her uneasiness about being so demanding—not wanting to give up one of her meetings—and her guilt feelings for asking people to go out of their way for her. What emerged through the fantasy exercise, however, were a whole set of other feelings that were poised just behind her guilt.

Jennifer contacted her feelings of resentment towards Bob for leaving the arrangements in her hands. At first, she hadn't felt she had a right to be angry with him, because she hadn't protested against the situation in the first place. She felt she had colluded in a dynamic between them that rested on the (unstated) premise that she was the one who should be responsible for Rachel, and that Bob's activities had a right to take precedence over hers. The incident pinpointed both their roles in the set-up. If she didn't stand up for herself, Bob would act in an unthinking way; she would then sacrifice what she wanted and end up feeling guilty for wanting what was legitimately hers in the first place.

These kinds of feelings and the paths they travel will be part of what you will be exploring as you work on your compulsive-eating problem. Coming in contact with your inner feelings can be an exciting, relieving, painful and reassuring process. It is always preferable to try to come to grips with your inner life, because feelings are insistent. If they are buried, as they are so frequently in compulsive eating, they can motivate us in ways of which we are unaware. We then find ourselves doing and saying things that seem inappropriate and confusing. As we begin to know more about our feelings, we can make more sense of who we are.

To work on expressing your feelings in appropriate, satisfying ways, turn to the exercise on page 141.

Coping with "Difficult" People

It is inevitable that, within each group, the people will take on different roles and responsibilities, even in a situation where there is equality of experience. However much emphasis we put on structuring the group as an equal and safe environment, everyone is unique and the combination of each person's uniqueness shapes a group and gives it its particular flavor. Because you are embarked on an experiment to help you focus on aspects of what makes you tick, you will be using the group to explore your individuality, what makes you who you are, and the kinds of experiences that have led you (unconsciously) to eat compulsively as a way of coping and using your body size to express yourself. This is different from a consciousness-raising group, where the stress is on the similarity of women's experiences so as to pinpoint the ways society affects us all as women.

Tensions can arise in a group situation because of the gap between the type of person you are in the world—for example, spontaneous, passive, organizing or whatever—and the part of you that needs to be explored in order for you to get over your compulsive-eating problem. In a group you will need to call on a different part of yourself. You will be encouraging the reflective, patient and empathetic aspects of your personality to develop so that you can come in contact with the deep feelings that cause you to eat compulsively.

It may be that your group includes a member who has such difficulty finding this part of herself that she acts in ways that feel unproductive to the group. Some groups have consulted with me over what to do when they find one of their members is disruptive, domineering or bossy in the group.

This is an extremely difficult situation to face and you may find yourselves trying to ignore the problem or "forgetting it," hoping that it will just go away or that the difficult person will leave town unexpectedly. It may take a while for these feelings to be verbalized among group members and, most often, these communications happen outside of group meetings while you are chatting on the way home in twos and threes.

The group already described contacted me for advice on just this problem. The matter had come to a head for them during one group session when Belinda was absent. The session proceeded very smoothly, and the last fifteen minutes or so people opened up to each other that they had felt particularly relaxed that evening and able to work together in a more trusting atmosphere than usual. Realizing how comfortable they were with each other that evening, they were starkly confronted with the question of how much Belinda's presence contributed to the tension and occasional anger that ordinarily existed in the group.

Several women then mentioned that they had been thinking of leaving the group because they found her overbearing and somehow frightening.

They felt extremely uncomfortable and somewhat guilty discussing this without Belinda, while realizing that they never could have had the discussion in her presence. Before doing anything—saying anything to Belinda—they decided to see whether they weren't each individually making Belinda into a scapegoat for their own problems.

Being in a self-help group can be difficult because it is such a new experience, and it can be as confusing as it is exciting. Everyone was very wary of casting Belinda in the role of the person who made the group difficult for them, because each member realized that she had to be responsible for trying to work on her compulsive-eating problem as effectively as possible in the group setting. However, the relief that all of them felt on this occasion led them to ring me and ask for advice.

As I listened to two of them on the telephone, it sounded to me very much as if Belinda, very energetic but unable to work on her own eating problems, was transforming that energy into almost taking over others' problems, being over-involved with them, and being pushy with her own ideas about what they needed to do for themselves. It struck me that perhaps she was afraid of the things that were inside of her, of her emotional life, and that her dominating personality both covered her vulnerabilities and pushed the attention on to others' emotional problems and away from herself, while still keeping her in the picture.

The group decided that the best thing for them to do would be to try and talk through these issues with Belinda at the next session, and they decided to be open-minded about where that might take them. Their intention was to fill her in on what they had noticed about the group session without her. They were very gentle and not at all judgmental, taking on to themselves the responsibility for not having cut her off in the past when they had found her comments unhelpful. They shared with her how they felt—that she was charismatic and powerful, that it was partly their problem that they didn't intervene differently or relied too much on her energy, and that they felt they could hide their lack of therapy skills behind her knowledge.

Belinda was shaken by all of this but also relieved, because she recognized that she was acting in this group as she had in many other settings. She had a tendency to take over and people saw her as quite dazzling and strong, and yet she felt small inside—ineffectual and as though her own needs went unaddressed. She shared with the group just how vulnerable and hopeless she did feel, and she said she worried that if she exposed herself in the group she would make everyone else feel as helpless as she did.

For the first time, Belinda revealed the anguish that her compulsive eating and her fat caused her. As she opened up to herself, her own pain, the rest of the group was overwhelmed by it as she had anticipated. But they were also moved and felt much closer to her, and they were able to reassure Belinda that they could understand *her* and help *her* too.

During the course of the evening they discussed the ways Belinda avoided her own experience and jumped into someone else's, and how they might all together try to intervene in that process so that she could get more out of the group for herself without invading other people's space. They committed themselves to seeing how this would work for four sessions, and everyone agreed to be aware of the dynamic in which Belinda lunged with her energy into another person's problem, leaving that person feeling pushed out of shape.

Belinda's commitment was to notice when she felt inclined to do that and to intervene as soon as she could identify that she was doing it. Instead, she was to try and contact the part of her that was feeling vulnerable or identified with what another woman might be exposing about herself. The woman who felt invaded was to say so as soon as possible, so that she could ensure that her space was not taken up by Belinda's needs and could also alert Belinda to when she was being unhelpful.

In this group, an extremely good result emerged. The group was solid enough to handle Belinda's upset and give her a sense of the possibilities that lay in the group for her. But this is not always the case, and it may be that a group has to come to a more difficult decision that the members feel very tortured about.

My advice to groups which contain a member who is disliked or found difficult by other group members is as follows:

1. First examine why you find this member difficult. Is it her? Is she controlling? Bossy? Always inappropriate? Is she overbearing? Is it a case of identification? What are her problems with compulsive eating? Do they remind you of your own? Is she a scapegoat?

2. Can you think of how to change the dynamic? Will she benefit by your sharing your insights with her, or would it only be hurtful?

Set aside a time to be open with her, telling her of your experience of her. Perhaps she needs additional help such as one-to-one therapy. Perhaps she is very ambivalent about being part of the group at this stage. Perhaps she isn't ready to work on her compulsive-eating problem. See if you can't all come up with a solution together that would make it possible for her to stay in the group and work with herself differently. If this is not possible, consider taking the hard step of asking her to leave. There is a real danger that an entire group will be worn away by frustration through trying to cope with such a difficult situation. But asking her to leave will be quite hard, and it may bring up complicated feelings for all the remaining members of the group.

It is important to talk these feelings out with each other should you face that decision, so that it can be a group responsibility. In most situations, while several group members may feel strongly about such a move there will also be several others who feel too uncomfortable to act on it. This can then produce a sort of no-go situation in which people are less conscientious about coming to the group, put less energy into it when they are there, and the group withers away through attrition. Several members may then regroup and start up again.

"Difficult" group members come in different personalities, and how they interact with other members can cause friction, upset and misunderstanding. One group may be quite comfortable with someone whom another group finds hard to integrate.

A group with one very reticent member who always talks last and hopelessly, may find her "difficult." They may experience leaving meetings on a down note and feel as though they haven't been able to give anything to her. I would advise such a group to make an effort to help this person talk earlier on in the evening and encourage her to focus on why she feels it is so hard to be given to. Another group may become terribly irritated by a member who doesn't speak to the point, overruns her time and is generally unable to discipline herself.

To try to alleviate this and similar problems, I suggest building in regular assessments of the group process during which matters of timekeeping and general group functioning can be discussed. This doesn't have to take up more than, say, twenty minutes every six or eight sessions, but it is a way to air problems that are bound to come up in any compulsive-eaters group. It can also provide a space for group members to discuss worries and concerns that do not have a place in the regular work of the group. It is during these assessments that the discussions can cover plans for special group activities, the issue of bringing in new members, or complicated feelings between two group members that are not disruptive to the group as a whole but are painful for the individuals involved.

A self-help group works well on compulsive eating as long as it focuses on the topic at hand and each individual's relationshp to compulsive eating. The group tends to be much less useful if it gets involved in the dynamics between group members, which usually means a turn away from the purpose of the group. To explore complicated group dynamics in this setting can serve the individual members as a defense against working on the issues at hand—compulsive eating, fatness and slimness. (If you are interested in exploring the dynamics that develop between group members, I suggest you join a general therapy group where such themes are the focus of the group.)

Intensity and Boredom

At times, like anyone else, whether in a group or working on your own, you will go through ups and downs, boredom, times of despair, and so on. Nor is every time you sit down to work going to be automatically exhilarating. In fact, there can be weeks on end when it just feels like hard work or doesn't seem to make much sense.

Almost everyone goes through periods of boredom when they feel discouraged and may even think of abandoning the approach or dropping out. Nothing seems to be happening, and you feel energyless. In itself, I don't think this phenomenon is entirely negative. For linked to the compulsive-eating syndrome is an almost equally compulsive tendency to see things in extreme terms—either you are great or awful, either you are a star or buried deep within a crowd. Events are either smashing or terrible. In other words, life is experienced only with intensity; the texture of ordinariness is never investigated for what it might have to offer.

Curiously, this very intensity is a kind of deprivation, for it obliterates crucial dimensions of human experience. It is almost as though the person is not sure of her existence if she is neither suffering acutely nor ecstatically happy. This is reflected at the food level, where the compulsive eater is habituated to eating in dramatic ways, either bingeing or depriving herself.

Experiencing ordinariness, boredom, frustration and discouragement can be helpful. You are learning to tolerate these kinds of feelings without rushing away from them and drowning yourself in frantic activity, deep depression or filling the space by eating. In living through these feelings and accepting them, you can begin to have a sense of yourself as surviving and existing in an undramatic emotional environment. This begins to alleviate the need to be always intensely involved in a compulsive way. In accepting these moods, we can become less afraid of them and explore them for what they are. Often the psychological profile of a compulsive eater expresses a deep need to run away from the more pedestrian aspects of daily life. But these times have their own pleasures if we know how to listen for them, just as ripples in a sea have their own beauty distinct from the dramatic intensity of crashing waves.

When these unremarkable patches occur, it is useful to note your own reactions to them and to see how the situation affects you. It may be that you are learning to express a side of your personality that has long been buried, the side that is not always sparkling or interesting or making sure that everyone is all right; the side that is sitting quietly and going along with what is happening, not having to initiate action or whip up energy out of a fear of being with yourself.

This learning to sit with yourself and be inside your own skin in a calm way is not to be confused with another feeling that often can set in, which is a feeling of boredom or passivity when you don't feel you can risk really exploring what your food problems are about. It is important to remember, in these cases, that your boredom may well be a way of fending off the changes that might result from purposeful work on your food problem.

Creating Psychological Safety

Sometimes the energy flows out of the room and the atmosphere is one of depression and keeping things down. In other words, there is an almost tangible feeling of suppression, like the closeness of a humid day. This can happen when you and your partner or all the members of a group are so afraid of looking into your food problems that you park your energetic selves at the front door before you start a session, and you transmit to one another wordlessly a sort of "keep-off" warning that is hard to break through. The best thing to do in those circumstances is to acknowledge that they exist. If the mood persists for several weeks and you don't seem able to generate any energy, then there may not be enough safety in the situation to open up.

This sometimes happens if you feel, even if you don't articulate it to yourself, that the hour or two that you have set aside each week for working on the problem isn't really enough. Opening up under such circumstances may make a person feel too vulnerable, especially if she feels that what she might have to expose about herself (and *to* herself) is her neediness. In many groups, women have found it helpful to make arrangements to have phone contact with each other between group sessions. In a group that starts off composed of strangers, this might need to be instituted, rather than hoping that it will just happen. If you're working on your own, perhaps you could invite a trusted friend to join you and support you in exploring your fears (it is much better if she also has a food problem).

For example, some women may not feel they can open up because they fear they will lose control. Such a woman may feel that her problem is so big that neither she nor anyone else can handle it. If she were to make arrangements to phone different friends or other group members each night of the week, say, and discuss with them how her day had gone in terms of her emotions and her eating, she might feel sufficiently supported to try new things out. Most people would not consider such arrangements a burden and are happy to make themselves available to each other provided they feel clear about exactly what it is they are being asked to give.

Other strategies that can be useful for groups include planning special sessions to last five hours or more, in which everyone has much longer to work on her problems and to pursue issues that perhaps don't emerge in shorter weekly group sessions.

CHAPTER 7

Organizing a Compulsive-Eating Group

Getting Started

There can be many stumbling blocks to overcome when grappling with compulsive-eating problems. Partly this stems from a disbelief and despair that anything can change, partly from the difficulty of coping directly with a whole range of emotional issues and partly it is a reflection of a dynamic of the problem itself—namely, the difficulty with being persistent and openly responsible for our food intake.

For many women, getting involved in a compulsive-eaters group will be their first experience of therapy. They may have lots of ideas about such a group but feel hesitant about how to put the concepts in *Fat Is A Feminist Issue* into practice. These two issues—the compulsive-eating problem itself and inexperience in therapy—can join together and translate into difficulties in organizing groups. This section is an attempt to share the information we have been accumulating at The Women's Therapy Centre about compulsive-eaters groups so that you will have a chance to benefit from that experience and see if any of the difficulties you might be coming up against have been solved by other groups.

For some women, the problem starts with not knowing how to get in touch with a group, or how to get one going if there are none in their area. The first step is to go to your local women's center and find out if a compulsive-eaters group already exists. There are so many groups now that the odds are you will be able to make contact this way. If you can't locate an existing group the next step may be to put up notices in obvious places—doctors' offices, colleges and in the local newspaper calling for a meeting at a specific time and place. This seems preferable to just giving a telephone number and collecting names, for several reasons. People are able to set aside a specific date to attend, you won't be juggling other people's schedules in your head, and it minimizes the difficulties that may arise in relation to leadership of the group.

When you have come together for your first meeting you will want to explain to each other why you are interested in being involved in a group to tackle compulsive eating. Find out if there is indeed a common interest. You may want to share your own experience with food and discuss what appealed to you in this approach.

Depending on the group's familiarity with the ideas in *Fat Is A Feminist Issue,* you may be able to start your group therapy at the first meeting. If people are new to the ideas, it will make sense for them to first familiarize themselves with the book so that they can be sure they are committing themselves to something they want. This also helps keep the original organizer of the group from getting trapped into being a leader because she has more knowledge of the theories.

This is an important point, because it is quite hard to lead a group *and* be in it for yourself. An ex-compulsive eater can be enormously helpful in enabling a new group to get off the ground, but a person who wants a group so that she can work on her own problems with food and body image would be well-advised *not* to see herself as a leader just because she is an initiator. This is to be a self-help group, which means that you as a group will need to share the commitment for making it happen. It isn't helpful to rely on one person. So, at this first meeting, make it clear that you have organized the getting together but are not in a position to lead the group, and that as a group you will evolve a collective sense of responsibility and leadership.

Once you have assembled a group (six to ten members seem like the right number) you will find it helpful if you not only set a regular meeting time and place but also make an initial commitment of meeting weekly for six months. This time commitment will allay your fears of sharing intimate things about yourself one week and receiving no response or support the following week. It also forces the group to confront a perhaps uncomfortable fact. For most people this approach does not produce instant results. It takes time to eat differently and feel differently in your body. Don't underestimate it. Give yourself and the group a chance to be helpful for all of you.

When you make your six-month commitment, try to be there every time and make sure you contact someone if you have to miss a session unexpectedly. If you are having difficulty getting to the group or if you feel nervous about the issues that are coming up for you, see if you can share this with the group so that they can provide gentle support.

Finding a Place to Meet

There are so many unanticipated problems that can come up in this kind of experimental group that the more you can plan for, the better are your chances of group survival. So, for example, it's a good idea to set a regular meeting place; or, if that doesn't suit group members, plan in advance where the group will be meeting so that there is no anxiety about where the sessions will take place. It is best to work within a fairly small geographical area so that traveling distances don't become a reason not to make a group meeting when you are finding it hard for emotional reasons to get to the group.

Through the questionnaire sent out by The Women's Therapy Centre, we found that some women like to meet in each other's homes on a rotating basis; others like the anonymity of a room booked from a church hall or community center. In groups that included several mothers, baby-sitting sometimes proves to be a problem, so those groups often met in the homes of those with young children. It is not important which system you choose, but it is important that the group members are comfortable with the system, know where the meetings are going to be, and make the commitment to start the meetings on time.

Planning the First Sessions

After you have set a time and a place, you will want to plan for your first few meetings. In these first weeks you will be feeling each other out, getting a sense of one another, a new sense of yourself and beginning the process of building sufficient safety and trust to open up the painful issues that are involved in your compulsive eating. In the chapter on self-help in *Fat Is A Feminist Issue*—which I recommend you all read before the second group meeting—I have laid out some exercises designed to help each person pinpoint underlying themes that are expressed in their eating. Two of these exercises are reproduced in the back of this book in slightly different forms. They are the "Fat/Thin" exercise and the "Supermarket Fantasy." As your group progresses, an almost infinite number of topics will evolve that you will want to discuss.

You may wish to start off your first group meeting by going round the room, with each person taking 10 to 15 minutes to introduce herself and share the history of her food problem. Of course, we could all talk for hours and hours about the ins and outs of our individual food histories, but here in this first exercise you should be trying to achieve certain things. One, you are presenting information about yourself in a selective and purposeful way—not rambling on, trying to find or avoid the point, but rather searching to put into words the painful story of your relationship to your body and your food over the years. Try to convey the feelings about how having a food problem affected you in the past and in the here and now. Try to sort out when you first noticed that you had a problem around food. How, or through whom, did you become aware of it? What was the extent of your family's involvement? Did food become a battleground at home? Was it a hidden problem? Did you have friends who had similar problems? Were you always dieting? Did you ever reach the weight you felt pleased about? What happened when you were your ideal weight? How did you feel climbing up the scale, and so on.

Secondly you are trying to see whether any patterns or insights emerge for you about yourself and your eating by looking over the long term. Thirdly, you are learning to talk in a supportive environment about issues that may be very hard for you to face. Everyone in the group has a difficult history with food and can therefore be understanding. You will have some time to talk and to be listened to without interruption so that you will hear your words reverberate back and begin to notice what is significant for you.

As presenting your food problem will undoubtedly bring up much more than can be covered in 15 minutes, you may wish to carry on with this exercise at home. You may find it helpful to take another period of time, say up to an hour, when you are on your own to reflect on what meaning this history has for you. You may wish to talk into a tape recorder, and just meander leisurely back over your experiences, or you may want to write your observations down in a journal. The method you choose for work outside of the group should be one that suits you best.

After everyone has had a chance to talk, the group may wish to spend 10 to 15 minutes at the end of the group time sharing the common themes that emerged, identifying with each other, commenting on anything you noticed about each other's stories that might be insightful and helpful. You should then plan for who will tape the fantasy for next week. I suggest you start with the "Fat/Thin" exercise, and then in your third week do the "Supermarket Fantasy."

When you come to the group meeting hungry for attention, it can be hard if your turn doesn't come up for some time. Or you may arrive feeling you have nothing to say, and this can be a form of resistance, often related to being scared of what is on your mind. If the group then goes on for an hour or so before your turn comes up, you could become even more withdrawn. In order to avoid these problems, I suggest starting each group session off so that each member has a chance to talk in the first fifteen minutes.

At the beginning of the meeting, decide on one person to be time-keeper for the session (this should be a revolving job). Divide up into pairs for a short period of co-counselling, which the timekeeper will direct by suggesting that those who talk first should tell the listeners what is on their minds about food and body image. When five or seven minutes is up, the timekeeper should tell you to swap roles. Having a chance to talk early on in the session can lessen problems of resistance, impatience, or not knowing what you want to talk about. It can also form a clear boundary between your activities of the day, including getting to the meeting, and the work you will be doing on compulsive eating.

After the ten or fourteen minutes is up and each person has had a chance to speak and a chance to listen, I suggest you sit silently for a minute or so to reflect on how you would like to use your time that evening. Would you like to pursue something that came up for you during the co-counselling, or are you aware that another theme is actually more pressing? Be clear what your intentions are for the session, and decide what makes most sense for you.

In the second part of the session the timekeeper might begin by asking who would like to talk first. In some groups, members find that choosing an order to go in ensures that everyone talks, including those who are shy. Some groups are especially sensitive to members who hold back and encourage them to speak early on in the session so that waiting doesn't build up extra nervousness. Other groups have found that acting spontaneously but keeping aware of who tends to talk at the beginning—and making sure the less assertive get their chance too—works well.

The aim is not to bludgeon members into baring their souls, but to make it safe and comfortable enough for everyone to talk freely about food, fatness and thinness. In order to create that space, it is helpful that each member's time be hers to be used as she wishes, rather than making her stick rigidly to a pre-arranged topic or activity unless it is relevant to everyone.

In structuring the sessions, I recommend dividing the time equally among group members. Sharing the time from the beginning can obviate some of the problems that have cropped up before in self-help groups. It minimizes the possibility of some members dominating the others and provides a mechanism to cope with imbalance if it occurs. It also places the responsibility for the group—and hence individual progress—on each person, thus undercutting the problems that can arise when people seek or offer leadership.

Sometimes in a group it feels as though things would be smoother, sticky patches would be unstuck more easily, if there were a group leader to give guidance and direction. Unthinkingly, participants may transfer those leadership expectations to one or two group members, and, in each group, there may well be one or two women who accept that role. However, this is often not a useful development, especially for the designated "leaders," because they may find themselves with skills that they can use with others without this attention being reciprocated. In addition, if a leadership expectation is set up, it will be very easy for group members to become disappointed when the unspoken leader lets them down.

In self-help you will be learning about yourselves and how to help others simultaneously. The group will be strengthened by each person developing a confidence that she could be a leader. To encourage this, you may wish as individuals or as group representatives to attend workshops on therapy skills and then bring them back to the group. You may wish to do some reading about self-help, and you will definitely find Sheila Ernst's and Lucy Goodison's book *In Our Own Hands: A Book of Self-Help Therapy* (Houghton, Mifflin, Boston, 1981) very useful. It is full of suggestions and examples of how to do self-help therapy. However, bear in mind that yours is a focused group, and that you must not lose sight of your goals regarding food and body image.

What to Do When People Leave the Group

People leave a group for a variety of reasons. Some will leave because they feel they have conquered the problem; others will leave because they don't feel ready to engage with the problem at the level required; and some others will leave because they feel hopeless. It is a good idea when planning to leave a group to discuss your reasons with the group members to see if, having spoken aloud about it, you still feel the same way. You can also work out a timetable for leaving that seems appropriate. The person who is leaving may feel overjoyed, scared, grateful, disappointed, angry or discouraged. There are bound to be reactions stirred up in the remaining group members, which can range from abandonment or fear to relief or anger.

Because at such a moment in the life of the group there are so many feelings flying around, it is a good idea to set a time aside to express them. Those who leave because they have done well will want the group's support and blessing. Those who are left may want to discuss new issues that crop up for them, such as feeling over-responsible for the group, feeling that to question the workings of the group would jeopardize its very existence, or feeling pressure to produce interesting things to talk about each week in order to keep other people interested and so on. Make sure this extra time is added to each person's personal allocation so that it doesn't take away from the direct work on compulsive eating that needs to happen each week.

Closed or Open Group

Obviously there are two choices in relation to whether your group should have an open-door policy in regard to new members or whether the group should become closed after it has stabilized its membership. The crucial factor to be considered is what will most contribute to a feeling of safety so that people can openly talk about their fears and desires, their conflicts and their anguish about food, fat and femininity.

We haven't accumulated decisive evidence in favor of either side of the question. Some groups report that they work best on a closed basis. The feelings of acceptance, encouragement and attentive listening come from the stability of the group, from getting to know each person well and being able to rely on the security that comes from continuity. Others have written to say that bringing in new members from time to time energizes the group; still others report that they have not been able to agree on this issue amongst themselves.

Each group will have to decide for itself. If there are disagreements among members, you may be able to resolve them through a third option—keeping the group closed for a certain period of time (say three months) and then opening it up to a new participant who is "interviewed" and accepted by all group members.

You may want to bring in more members for a variety of reasons. The group may be too small, a friend of one of the existing members may have become interested, or perhaps people have left the group. When a new member joins, the group will inevitably go through a period of adjustment. The newcomer can feel awkward, and a group that has become set in its ways will feel jolted. On the other hand, the entry of new members often produces an upswing in the energy level of a group that is very positive. The old group members have a chance to share the process they have been through together and, in explaining how the group works to a newcomer, they put into their own words what they have learned about themselves and about doing self-help therapy.

Because the course of a group can last several years, it is inevitable that its composition will change in that time. You may find yourself going through several phases in relation to this issue. One pressure that can arise towards including new members when you aren't seeking more is when there is no other group in your vicinity. News of your group and its work may bring you telephone calls and letters asking for help. I think the best thing to do in those circumstances is to see if there are two people in your group who would be willing to help another group get off the ground. They could, with the potential new members, call a meeting for interested people, share what they have learned so far and then leave it in the hands of the new group.

As compulsive eaters we have a tendency to try to absorb or accommodate ourselves to everyone else, even at the expense of our own needs. It is important to keep your needs in the foreground in this instance and not sacrifice your group security for the sake of being responsive to another sufferer. It is essential to draw the lines between you and others, strange as that may seem. So, in considering these issues, make sure you as a group are expressing what you as individuals most want and need.

Making It Work

The group can only work for you if you put a lot into it. There is a tremendous temptation to hope that, once you are in a group, your problems will just disappear. I cannot stress strongly enough that this will not happen. Only by active observation and intervention will your eating and body concepts shift.

Give yourself the time to work on the problem. Make your group session a priority event in your week; allow yourself to bring up your fears, despairs, frustrations, worries and advances in the group. Learn from your own experience and from each other.

Self-help groups can teach us a great deal about our inner lives and the richness they contain, which is often concealed by preoccupations with fat and compulsive eating. The atmosphere generated in many groups is one of tenderness, concern and purpose. Be patient with yourself and strive to get what you need for yourself from the group. And very good luck.

PART II

Psychological Exercises

How to Use the Exercises

Throughout the book you will have noticed the symbol ✷ referring you to this section of the book and to a particular exercise here. When you do these exercises, make sure you have plenty of time. Don't rush them; they will be of little benefit to you that way. When you plan to do an exercise, set aside a good half hour. This applies to all exercises except "Breaking Into a Binge," which you will find useful as a quick intervention if you are bingeing. Before you do any of the exercises, you might want to get yourself a blank 120-minute tape. Slowly read into your tape recorder the exercises, leaving good pauses where the dots are. As a rough guide, each exercise takes about seven to ten minutes to tape. You may prefer to ask a friend to do this for you or you may wish to send for a prerecorded tape I have made of some of the exercises (available for $5 from Tapes, Suite 101, 80 East 11th Street, New York, NY 10003). Whatever method you choose, you will find it extremely helpful to be able to close your eyes and listen to a tape rather than having to interrupt your fantasies to read the exercises.

Sit down in a comfortable chair with the tape recorder close at hand so that you can turn it on and off without moving from the chair.

Stay in your chair and sit quietly after you turn off the tape before you go on to the questions that follow several of the exercises.

The exercises are designed to help you consider aspects of your emotional life in a new way. I have attempted to help you create different scenes in your imagination by feeding in various ideas from which you can take off. Not everyone has an easy time fantasizing at first (although many women love it straight off) and some women say they feel a bit silly initially; some balk at the idea of sitting quietly, eyes shut, doing a guided fantasy. Most often what prevents us from getting into fantasizing in this way is a nervousness or embarrassment about letting ourselves go or a worry that we aren't doing it right. Sometimes you may notice that, instead of pursuing the fantasy I have tried to outline for you, your mind is wandering off in an altogether different direction and you can feel confused about what to do. You may not be able to fantasize at all and feel distracted by the unrelated thoughts that zoom through your mind. You may find yourself tuning into the fantasy halfway through or intermittently; the long pauses between the short phrases are there to help you relax and create whatever mental images you can. A woman who does the exercises in a group can feel a bit uncomfortable if she comes up with a less elaborate fantasy than the other members, but in all of these reactions the important thing to do is to *stay with your experience, try not to panic, and be as open as you can* to whatever—however off the topic it may seem—floats through your mind. Don't be discouraged if you don't have a rich fantasy the first time you attempt one.

The more you do the fantasies the more you will get out of them and the more attuned your mind becomes to doing them. Each time you do one you will notice that you can gather new information about yourself. Sometimes the differences will be almost imperceptible, at other times you will be astonished at how varied your responses can be.

✸　THE IDEAL KITCHEN

Sit down, get comfortable, and relax. I'd like you to
close your eyes and imagine that you are contentedly
on your own for a couple of days at a rather magical
place that has everything you would possibly
want.... Take your pick of location—sun, sea, moun-
tains, forest, city...whatever really pleases you.... You
are staying in a little apartment that is part of a beau-
tifully designed holiday complex. Each apartment has
its own kitchen, although you can order anything you
like from a main kitchen to be brought to your room
or you can eat in a public dining room.... Soak in as
many details as possible of this gorgeous holiday spot
where you've chosen to be for a couple of days on
your own.... Now I'd like you to go into the kitchen
in your apartment and just take a look at the supplies
that have been laid out for you.... Remember, this is
a magical place, so you won't be at all surprised to find
your most favorite foods are there.... As you inspect
the fridge, the fruit bowl, the cheese tray, the cookie
tin, the bread board, and so on, you notice how very

well the food has been chosen for you.... How does seeing all this food in this setting make you feel?... Perhaps you sigh contentedly, perhaps you feel overwhelmed, perhaps you feel safe.... While you are looking at the food and experiencing your feelings and enjoying being on your own, imagine that you leave the food temporarily to run yourself a bath.... In the fantasy the bath is now full and I'd like you to get into it and relax.... Feel the pleasure of being in this place with all your favorite foods put there especially for you.... Focus on the positive aspects.... Lie˙back in your bath and give yourself enough time to see what it is you feel like doing as soon as you are out of the bath.... Are you hungry?... If so, what would you like to eat and how?... Do you wish to be on your own or with other people? See what feels absolutely right for you.... Having thought through what would suit you best.... Now imagine yourself eating if you *are* hungry.... Perhaps you aren't inclined to eat right now but want to take a nap, sunbathe, chat with someone, swim, ski, read, walk, watch TV; see what it is you would really like to do, and in your mind's eye, pursue the activities that feel right to you.... Nobody else's needs will intrude here; you can really choose what is exactly right for you.... Reflect on how it feels to know that, when you are hungry, you will have a gorgeous treat awaiting you.... Now I'd like you to stay in that frame of mind but bring yourself back to the here and now and consider the possibility of giving yourself the exact food you are longing for when you next get hunger signals.... Can you do that?... If it seems difficult, is it because you feel money is standing in your way?... Think through your food budget and see whether you couldn't cut down on something else that you don't really enjoy in order to buy some of what you want.... Do you feel you are not entitled to the foods you really want?... Try and feel any resistances you might have to looking after yourself well with food.... Now imagine that you are free of any impediment to enjoying the food.... How does that make you feel?... Now rouse yourself out of the fantasy and come back to the room you're sitting in. Open your eyes and do something you find relaxing—you can just stay in your chair if you wish, or you might want to take a bath for real.... Choose an activity that will allow you to think for another few minutes uninterruptedly. If you're using a tape, turn off the cassette while you do this. When you are ready, return to this exercise. Sit down and close your eyes again and reflect back over the last twenty-four minutes of your life. See if you can pinpoint those occasions when your eating satisfied and pleased you and those when it didn't.... Try to figure out why your eating wasn't satisfying.... Was it the food, was it the people, was it the way you ate?... As you are relaxing, be aware of as many details of each eating situation as you can.... Now turn your attention to the foods you would like to have in your kitchen now, and what you would most like to eat.... Try and stay with this feeling, picking out the exact food or beverage you would really like.... When you are ready, open your eyes, and refer to the questions that follow this exercise.

❉

1. How do you feel about the food in your own kitchen at present?

2. Does it include foods that you especially like?

3. What are your favorite foods? Are they new discoveries? Are they foods from your childhood? Make a list. Do you have particular moods that go with particular foods?

4. How did you feel with all your favorite foods in the holiday apartment?

5. Do you like anticipating what you will eat the next time you are hungry, or do you gain more satisfaction by spontaneously responding to that hunger? Remember your favorite foods for those occasions when you are hungry but don't know what to eat.

6. Does having nice food worry or upset you? If so, what do you fear it will do to you?

❋ BREAKING INTO A BINGE

Sit down, close your eyes, and take a few deep breaths.... The fact that you have been able to pry yourself away from the food to listen to the tape is a big step in the direction of breaking away from your binge. Try and feel the relief of having interrupted the binge.... Now I'd like you to think back to when you were first aware that you were going to be eating this way on this occasion.... Did it start before you even began to eat, or did it flow out of a satisfactory, or perhaps unsatisfactory meal?... Bring to mind all the details... where you were, who you were with, the general atmosphere.... Try and pinpoint the sensation you experienced in the binge.... What foods did you go for?... Were you concentrating on taste or texture or was the food eaten in such a way that you couldn't discriminate?... Were you looking for something?... Were you depriving yourself of a particular food that you finally succumbed to or does it feel more as though you were trying to avoid some feelings?... What is it that you are searching for in the food?... Try and feel what it is that you really want.... Try to put that wanting into words or into an image.... Feel again the relief of having torn yourself away from the binge.... What can you do now to give yourself something more truly nourishing?... Do you want to have a cry, a bath, a nap?... Do you want to reach out to someone... write to them or ring them?... Do you want a hug from someone special?... Try and find an appropriate response to your longing.... Don't deny the longing, even if you can't find the right response.... Try and accept it. It won't eat you up, above all don't expect the food to satisfy it.... Be aware of your emotional hunger and take a few moments to let yourself experience it directly.... Decide in a relaxed way what you'd like to do after finishing this exercise and, when you are ready, open your eyes.

❀

❈ INCREASING YOUR FOOD AWARENESS

Close your eyes and get comfortable.... In this fantasy you will have the chance to go through a few minutes of your past again, and increase your awareness of your food habits.... Remember back to the most recent time this week that you either ate more than you were wanting or that you were drawn to eating and started to eat but knew you weren't hungry.... It will help you to recreate the feelings if you remember the details and particulars of the situation.... Were you on your own or with others, in your kitchen or in a public place?... Draw the scene as vividly in your mind's eye as you can, so that it's as though you were observing a film of yourself in the situation.... And now I'd like you to replay the incident slowly, frame by frame.... Start by focusing on what was happening just before you ate when you weren't really hungry.... Does the scene feel familiar?... Is this the time you usually overeat?... Is this one of those persistently difficult times you have around food?... Had you prepared to eat or did you just sort of stumble into the refrigerator or candystore

137

or whatever?...Were you at a friend's house and didn't know how to, or feel able to refuse her offer of food?...Now that you've set the scene, focus in on the emotional state just before you ate....How were you feeling?...Can you give your feelings a name?...Let whatever feelings you were having then come to the surface now....Carefully consider those feelings before moving on in this exercise....Now, I'd like you to imagine you are eating the food. What are you eating? As methodically as you can, see how much of the food you actually tasted, at what point you felt physically full, and how long you continued to eat after that point....Were you grabbing desperately for the food or were you eating calmly?...See if you can come up with words that precisely describe the way you were eating....See if you can distinguish exactly what kind of satisfaction you were getting from the food....Now I'd like you to return to the point *before* you started to eat or found yourself eating more than you were needing....Focus in on your emotional state....If you can't quite get it into focus, think back over the various incidents of the day up until that point and see if you can recapture how you felt....Was it a day when your emotions were seesawing?...Did you receive some disappointing news?...It's even possible, of course, that everything was going well before you ate....There are no formulas here; just take your time to see what you were actually feeling....Now I'd like you to imagine that, instead of eating or overeating, you stay in this emotional state....See if you can replay the scene from this point on, except this time allow yourself to not eat....Give yourself time to live through any immediate anxiety that not eating might produce, and see what then comes up for you.... Are you being overwhelmed by uncomfortable feelings, or is not eating much less difficult than you had anticipated?... Allow yourself plenty of time to see what the desire for food may have been covering up in terms of other wishes....Allow yourself to be filled up with your emotions....Now gently rouse yourself from this exercise, open your eyes, and go back to the book.

�֍

❊ EXPRESSING YOUR FEELINGS

This exercise is designed to help you express your uncomfortable feelings in a way that feels right and satisfying to you. Close your eyes now and relax, and remember back to the last time you felt either angry, envious, competitive, jealous, sad, or depressed, and couldn't seem to get rid of the feeling. Choose any one of these feelings. When you do the exercise another time, you can choose another feeling. Having settled on which feeling you would like to explore, think over how often during the last few weeks you have felt this particular feeling and under what circumstances. ... Choose one of those times, preferably the one that is the most emotionally charged, and try to recapture in detail the surrounding circumstances that sparked off this feeling in you.... Who else was involved?... As you are recreating the scene, are you aware of wanting to dilute the feeling?... of judging yourself?... Are you blaming someone else?... Give yourself a chance to explore the reality of the situation and just notice the internal voices that interfere with your experiencing the feeling directly.... Do you often hold back from expressing to people what you are feeling?... Are you all choked up with feeling?... Imagine for a moment that you are able to say or express whatever you feel.... Imagine yourself telling whoever else is involved what impact they had on you.... If that feels impossible, try telling a friend about how this person made you feel.... Now try and tell the person directly.... Don't be apologetic, just tell them in a straightforward way about the impact the interaction had on you.... Don't allow yourself to get sidetracked into being oversensitive to what they might be feeling right now.... Focus instead on what *you* need to say to them.... See yourself doing it; it doesn't matter how many false starts you have.... Try again to express yourself as accurately and fully as you can.... How does it feel to be communicating your feelings?... How does it affect the picture you have of yourself?... Now think about whether you would actually like to tell this person in reality what you expressed during this fantasy.... Perhaps you'd like to write them a letter full of feelings, which you can choose to either send or not send.... Perhaps you'd like to tell them directly how they made you feel.... Sort out what feels right for you to do in order to feel satisfied and complete.... We are coming to the end of this exercise now, so see what you are able to take from it that you can use the next time these feelings well up in you.... Try to focus on one specific intervention that you feel you could use to express yourself, and when you are ready, open your eyes.

❉

❋ EXPLORING YOUR FEELINGS

Think about an emotion that is particularly troubling to you. What would you call this feeling? Is it anger, frustration, resentment, despair, guilt, competition, envy, jealousy, hatred, depression?... Now experience this feeling, and think back to what triggered it off.... Were you disappointed? Was it something someone said? Did the feeling come up because of something you felt unable to do?... Be aware of the circumstances that caused this feeling to erupt in you.... Do you have this feeling often?... What other kinds of situations can set off this feeling in you?... Allow yourself to experience the feeling as fully as you can.... What would you like to do right now?... See if you have any spontaneous urges to express this feeling—through crying, shouting, shaking or whatever.... Notice any thoughts going through your mind that interrupt your experiencing the feelings fully.... Let the thoughts pass quickly through your mind as you allow yourself to be aware of the intensity of your feelings.... As you are reliving the circumstances that

143

brought this feeling up in you, see if you can catch a whiff of any other feelings...perhaps feelings that are unfamiliar to you....Focus in on these feelings....Let them fill you up....Let go of all your thoughts and judgments, and let yourself experience your feelings fully....It's okay to be frightened of them—just try letting them come to the surface for a minute or two....You'll find that once you've actually experienced them, the feelings won't seem so scary....Remember that these are feelings you walk around with all the time. They are *already* a part of you. They have the power to confuse and frighten you only because they are usually hidden away....Allowing yourself the space to let them come up in this way shows you that you *can* handle them....Try and relax for a minute now....Think back over the feelings you have experienced during the course of this exercise...and concentrate on following your breathing, in and out, in and out.

❋

❀ FAT/THIN FANTASY

This exercise is designed to help you understand how you express yourself through your body and help you come to grips with the emotional issues you have attached to different body states. If you can do this exercise frequently it will provide you with a rich picture of the conscious and unconscious meanings of fat and thin for you. Since these meanings vary, and different moods can illuminate different meanings, the more often you do the exercise, the more you will get out of it. Now I'd like you to close your eyes, get as comfortable as you can, follow your breathing, in and out, in and out, and relax. I'd like you to imagine that you are at a party.... This can be either a real party or an imaginary one.... It might be a dancing party, a talking party, a small intimate party.... Set the scene and notice how you are feeling.... What are you wearing? ... How do you feel in these clothes?... Try and feel yourself in your body.... Now notice your behavior at this party. Are you an observer?... Are you actively mixing with other people; do you feel withdrawn?... As you observe yourself at this party, I'd like you to imagine that you are getting fatter.... You are now quite large.... How do you feel at this size?... Try and be aware of the nuances of feelings about being this size.... You may have both negative and positive feelings about being this size.... What are you wearing and how do you feel about your clothes?... What is going on at the party and how are you interacting with the other people there?... Are you on your own or are you talking, dancing, eating with others?... Do you feel comfortable or would you like to leave?... Can you initiate contact or do you feel you must wait until you are sought out?... Now I'd like you to imagine your fat is communicating with the people at the party.... It is saying something that I'd like you to put into words.... What is your fat saying to others?... Is there any way in which you feel it helps you to be *this* size in *this* situation?... Does being fat allow you to do or say certain things or act in particular ways?... Now imagine that your fat is peeling or melting away and, in this fantasy, still at the same party, you are now your ideal size.... Can you see yourself?... Can you feel yourself at your ideal size?... Notice what you are wearing.... What do these clothes say about you?... What do you see from the perspective of being your ideal size? ... Do you view the party with different eyes?... What or who do the people at the party see when they look at you?... How do you feel?... Are you sure of yourself or do you feel vulnerable?... How are you getting on with the others at the party?... Are there differences between how you interacted with people when you were fat and how you are getting on now?... What is the quality of your contact with others?... Focus on the positive feelings coming up in you about your being your ideal size.... Are you being seen as you?... Are you being admired for your body?... Now see if you notice any disconcerting feelings about being your ideal size at this party?...Is there anything scary or unpleasant about being this size?...Now I'd like you to imagine that you are fat once again, still at this same party....Does the atmosphere change?...How? ...How do you feel within yourself?...Can you contact any feelings of relief about being larger again?...Allow yourself time to experience whatever feelings are coming up. Notice your responses to other people and how you feel about yourself....See what messages this fat you is sending out....Is there any way in which it helps you to be fat at the party?...Are there any conflicts you seem able to avoid?...Are there some very private feelings concealed in the fat?...When you are ready, I'd like you to imagine that once again, at this party, you are your ideal size....How do you feel?...Allow yourself to experience the many complicated feelings you may have....Notice how you are in your "slim" clothes and how you feel in your body....Do you feel *you?*...Particularly note any difficult feelings that come up for you in being your ideal size....See if you can pinpoint any feelings that might have made it hard for you to stay at this size in the past....Now I'd like you to look back over this entire fantasy exercise and see what new information came up for you about yourself....When you are ready, turn to the questions below.

1. What positive aspects of fatness emerged that you hadn't realized you felt?

2. What emerged about aspects of your personality that you express through your fat?

3. How might you express that part of you if you were your ideal size?

4. What emerged about you at your imagined "ideal" size?

5. What fears came up for you about being slim?

6. What aspects of your personality are you currently suppressing that you imagine go with slimness?

7. How might you express those aspects now?

❁ MIRROR WORK

Sit down in the chair and close your eyes, follow your breathing for a moment and try to get a feel of your body from inside, and a mental picture of how you look sitting in the chair.... Imagine yourself as you are now and sit in a position that expresses how you feel about your body.... Now strike a confident pose... now an eager one... now an open attitude to the world... now a withdrawn stance.... Do all this with your eyes closed.... Just feel the internal changes and the shifts you are required to make.... Now I'd like you to imagine that you are your ideal size.... What are you spontaneously expressing in this pose?... Now try a series of poses just as you did before, only at your ideal size... open, withdrawn, eager, confident, reticent, and so on.... Notice how rich a repertoire of physical expression you have.... When you have familiarized yourself with the various feelings, review what was different about them at different imagined body sizes.... What aspects of the ideal size you would like to express right now?.... What are you afraid of, or what do you not want to express right now?...Did you discover anything at all difficult or surprising about feeling yourself into your ideal size?...Now open your eyes, stand up and take a good look at your whole body in the mirror....Follow the outlines of your body and get a picture of the whole of you rather than focusing in on details....Try not to judge, just look. Stand comfortably and try to project a feeling of accepting and liking yourself....Keep your back straight and turn sideways so that you get another picture of yourself....Just look, try not to judge....Now turn forwards and then to the other side....Just look, try not to judge....Turn forwards again and, starting with your toes, look all the way up your body and, when you reach your head, look from your head all the way down....As you look at yourself in the mirror, try to see yourself with accepting eyes....Turn to your right, stand as though you are now your ideal size and look into the mirror....Now turn to the other side....What do you see?...Now turn frontwards and resume your usual stance....What are the differences?...Now sit down on the chair as if you were your ideal size....What do you see?...How would it be for you to hold this position regularly?...Would it express more clearly how you feel about the inner you?...Would you appear to be too confident?...Hold this position for a minute and, when you are ready, go on to the questions below.

❋

Give yourself time to respond to these questions, as they can help you deepen your understanding of how you relate to your body.

1. Were you able to feel comfortable looking at yourself? Describe what you felt. As you do the exercise regularly, notice the small changes in self-acceptance.

2. What did you notice about the differences between the way you held your body to express the various emotional states? What did you notice when you tried to project yourself at your ideal size? What aspects of you came forward?

3. Try incorporating the positive aspects of how you hold your body at your ideal size into how you are in your body now. Start off by doing it for a few minutes each hour.

❋ PART OF THE BODY

I'd like you to lie down, get as comfortable as you can. Close your eyes and observe your breathing.... Try to feel your body physically.... Feel your breath as it travels through your body into your arms and legs, chest and diaphragm.... Now I'd like you to focus on the part of your body that you currently feel most unhappy about—it could be your legs, your stomach, your thighs, your breasts.... Review your feelings about this part of your body and see if you can get back to when you first became aware of it as a part of you that you weren't comfortable with.... Let whatever memories that come to mind emerge.... Now I'd like you to pinpoint what exactly it is about this part of you that you feel so rejecting of.... How would you describe that part of you?... What does that say about you?... What emotions is this part of your body expressing?... Now I'd like you to imagine that you are your ideal size.... What happens to this part of you?... Can you actually visualize how you would be or are you superimposing part of someone else's body

153

onto your own?...Are you seeing yourself as you once were?...Try and feel your body changing....If you really feel that this part of you would be more acceptable smaller, try to imagine yourself smaller and see how that feels....What does this part now express about you?...How do you feel in your body?...What does it mean to you not to have something you dislike about yourself to focus on?...Do you feel more comfortable or is there something strangely missing?...Let yourself experience whatever feelings come up in you whether they are positive, negative or confusing....Now I'd like you to go back to your body as it is in reality, including the part that gives you so much distress, and just feel it again....Do you get any further associations to this part and what you so dislike about it?...What does this expose about you?...Really let yourself explore this part of your body rather than judge it....Try and experience it as a part of you....Integrate it into the rest of your body....Now imagine again that you are your ideal size....What happens to this part of your body?...What does being your ideal size allow you to do in your imagination?...Do you approach the world differently?...Now think of a difficult situation you experienced this past week. Let the details of the situation come to life, and put yourself back into that situation but at your ideal size....Would it be different?...Really see how it would be and think it through....Now I'd like you to open your eyes and use the questions below to help you reflect on your experience in this exercise.

❀

1. What kind of associations did you come up with to this part of your body?

2. Do any other members of your family share the same concern about this part of their body?

3. If so, how do you feel about that part of their body?

4. Now spend some time exploring the themes that came up for you when you were doing the fantasy. Think through in detail your first awareness of your discomfort with this part of your body. What kind of role does this discomfort play currently, and what are the emotional issues this discomfort is masking? Are you perhaps assigning it more power than it has? Does being preoccupied with this part *help* you in any way?

5. Why do you so dislike this part? Is it because it doesn't conform to a stereotype? If in the fantasy you superimposed someone else's body part on to yours, whose was it—and what does that mean for you? If you saw yourself younger, what was so special about that particular time?

6. What is the actual bodily function of this part of your body? How well does it perform its physical function? How do you feel about its function?

❀ THE FAMILY MEAL

This exercise is designed to help you contact the emotional resonances of your childhood eating and to help you see how they affect your current eating patterns. Sit back, relax, close your eyes....Imagine that you are at a family dinner at your parents' home. It could be a special occasion, such as Christmas or a birthday. Choose a time when as many family members are there as possible....It could be a real situation or a fantasized one....If it helps you, remember back to a specific family occasion around the dinner table....Who is there?...How do people get on with each other?...Are there many sources of friction between the people? Are there unmentionable subjects and tense areas that everyone avoids, or do the tensions come to the surface?....Or is there perhaps a good feeling about all of you being together?...Notice the details of the situation and try to really feel yourself in the situation....Who do you feel closest to?...How does whatever is going on between people at the table get expressed through the food?...Notice how other people are eating.... Now notice what is going on for you with food.... How comfortable are you with your eating?... Really see yourself sitting there and describe your eating to yourself quickly and simply.... Now it's time for the dishes to be cleared away.... Who participates?... Who doesn't?... Is anyone eating what's been left over?... Observe yourself and your impulses.... Now I'd like you to remember back to when you were much younger, and conjure up a picture of your family's eating habits. What do you remember of them?... Paint the picture as vividly as you can.... Did you all eat together, or in separate shifts?... Did your mother do all the cooking?... Did you wish that she would behave differently in some way?... Did you wish that she would sit down more often?... Did she eat robustly, with pleasure, or pick at her food?... Were you encouraged to eat everything on your plate?... If you were, what would happen if you didn't?... Who served the food? Did each individual take their own, or did one of your parents serve you? Who decided what was the right size portion for you?... What was the atmosphere like at the table?... Did you look forward to mealtimes or not?... What happened there besides eating—was it a place for talking, shouting or disciplining?... Remember as many details as you can, both about the atmosphere and about how you and the other family members were eating.... Now I'd like you to think about your current eating situation in your present living arrangement.... What are meals like for you now?... What is the atmosphere like at the table? ... Who does the cooking?... How do you feel about that?... If you live alone, how do you feel about eating alone?... What do mealtimes mean to you?... Are they social occasions, a time of getting together, or are they fraught, or unpredictable, lonely or upsetting?... Be aware of the aspects of your mealtimes that give

you pleasure.... Now notice those aspects that cause
you discomfort.... Are there emotional continuities be
tween your present eating situation and the way you
felt as a child and as an adult about eating with your
family?... Reflect now on whether you may be trying
to make up for or trying to recreate the meals of your
childhood.... What are you looking for in a meal with
others?... Now think back to the tables you've been
fantasizing sitting at in the last few minutes and scan
them for anything else you may not have noticed the
first time.... How might you relate what you've noticed
about how you eat now and how you might want to
eat? When you are ready, open your eyes, and return
to the book.

❁

❊ THE CHINESE MEAL

Sit down, get comfortable and relax. Now I'd like you to imagine you are with a group of friends at a Chinese restaurant that you like.... How many people are at the table?... Do any of them have problems around food or are you the only one with a compulsive-over-eating problem?... Do you anticipate this communal meal with pleasure or nervousness or a mixture of both?... Use this opportunity to observe how you conduct yourself at such a meal, how you feel about the food on the table and how the other people handle this way of eating together.... How is the ordering done?... Does each person choose a dish for themselves, or to share, or is the whole menu decided by everyone together?... Do you feel comfortable or uncomfortable with the arrangement?... Are you participating actively in choosing the food?... Are you engaged in conversation?... Once the ordering is done, notice how you are feeling as you await the arrival of the food.... Are the ordered dishes mostly food that you like?... Are you worried about appearing

greedy?...Are you worried about overeating?...Are
you worried about not getting enough food?...The
food has now arrived....Does it all come at once or
one dish or two at a time?...Are the first dishes to
appear your favorites?...How are you feeling about
the food at this point?...Slow down....Take a few
deep breaths and think about the meal, alerting yourself to the areas that can cause you difficulty....Plan
how you could intervene at such times so that you
won't be eating in an unaware fashion; for example,
if you are inclined to put more food on your plate than
you really want to insure you get enough, and then
you habitually overeat rather than stop when you feel
satisfied, try a different response—either plan to observe your eating closely enough so that you are not
eating "unthinkingly," or take less food on your plate
initially and see how that feels....Do you feel deprived
or restricted?...As this is a fantasy, you can be absolutely sure that there will be plenty of food for you.
It will not run out. Bearing that in mind, how do you
feel putting smaller amounts on your plate, knowing
you can always take more?...Perhaps you'd prefer
to eat one dish at a time....In this fantasy you can tell
your friends that that is what you are doing and they
will make sure to leave you as much as you might want
of everything....What kind of feelings are you experiencing now?...Are you able to relax and enjoy the
food and taste each mouthful?...Can you distinguish
between the tastes you like and those you don't?...Try
and stay in touch with your eating as you socialize with
the people at the table....Now relax and continue with
the meal, only this time I'd like you to act as you usually
would on such an occasion....Now I'd like you to
reflect back on these last few moments: What was going
on for you?...How were you relating to the other
people and how did you feel about the way you were

eating?...See if you can spot moments of tension or compulsive eating....Focus now on any difficulties you're having....Try to replay that difficult part of the meal, but with your concentration turned to your eating....How might you be able to intervene differently?...You are now full....Has it been a satisfying or disappointing meal?...Notice the feelings in your body that let you know you've had enough food....Do you feel inclined to continue eating the food that is still on the table and perhaps in your dish, or are you quite content to stop?...If you are having difficulty stopping, try and put into a few words what you are still wanting....See if you can discover exactly what you want to best satisfy that hunger....What will you have to face if you stop eating when you are no longer hungry?...Now bring back the meanings and feelings of a communal meal like this for you. Do you feel mostly pleased, or mostly uncomfortable?...What would need to be happening around the table and in relation to the food to make it absolutely right for you?...Pinpoint whatever would make this a pleasant experience for you and consider what you could do the next time you have a meal like this....Remember what you did to intervene successfully when you felt like eating but were not hungry....When you are ready, open your eyes and reflect on the exercise.

❁ THE SUPERMARKET FANTASY

Close your eyes.... Now I would like you to imagine you are in your kitchen.... Look around the room and make a note of all the food there... in the refrigerator ... closets... cookie tin... freezer.... It probably is not too hard for you to form a complete picture because undoubtedly you know where everything is or is not, including any goodies or dietetic foods.... Look around the room and see how it is affecting you.... Is it painful to see how pathetic the foods are that you generally keep there or allow yourself to eat?... See what your kitchen says about you.... Now go to your favorite supermarket or shopping mall or a place where there is a wide variety of stores under one roof—vegetable market, butcher, delicatessen, dairy, bakery, take-out food store—and I would like you to imagine that you have an unlimited amount of money to spend.... Take a couple of supermarket carts and fill them up with all your favorite foods.... Go up and down the aisles or from counter to counter and carefully select the most appetizing foods.... Be sure not to skimp.... If you like cheesecake, take several, take enough so you feel that there is no way you could possibly eat it all in one sitting.... Be sure to get the specific ones you really like.... There is no hurry, you have plenty of time to get whatever you want.... Cast your eyes over the wonderful array of foods and fill up your cart.... Make sure you have everything you need and then get into your car or a cab with your boxes of food and go to your home.... There is nobody in the house and nobody will be around for the rest of the day; the house— especially the kitchen—is all yours for you to enjoy.... Bring the food into the kitchen and fill up the room with it.... How do you feel surrounded by all of this food just for you?... Does it feel sinful or is it a very joyful feeling?... Do you feel reassured or scared by the abundance of food just for you?... Just stay with the food and go through the various moods that come up.... Remember nobody will disturb you, the food is there just for you, enjoy it in whatever way you want to.... See if you can relax in the knowledge that you will never again be deprived.... And now I would like you to go down the road to mail a letter.... How do you feel about leaving the house and all the food?... Does it give you a warm feeling to know that when you go back it will all still be there for you undisturbed? Or is it a relief to get away from it?... You have now mailed the letter and are on your way back to the house.... Remember as you open the door that the food is all there just for you and no one will interrupt you.... How does it feel to be back with the food?... If you found it reassuring before, does it continue to be so? If you found it scary, can you find anything comforting about being back in the kitchen with all this food?... Slowly come back to the room you are actually in now with the knowledge that your kitchen is full of beautiful foods to eat that nobody is going to

take away from you... and, when you are ready, open
your eyes.

FOOD CHART

TIME OF DAY	CIRCUMSTANCES UNDER WHICH I APPROACHED FOOD: WAS I PHYSICALLY HUNGRY? IF SO, DID I ALLOW MYSELF A FREE CHOICE OF FOODS?	WHAT WAS I FEELING BEFORE EATING? WAS I EMOTIONALLY HUNGRY? IF SO, FOR WHAT?

WHAT AND HOW I ATE	DID THE FOOD SATISFY ME, OR NOT?	FEELINGS AFTER EATING

FURTHER READING

Boston Women's Health Book Collective. *Our Bodies Ourselves*. New York: Simon and Schuster, 1971.

Bruch, Hilde. *Eating Disorders: Obesity, Anorexia Nervosa and the Person Within*. New York: Basic Books, 1973.

Chernin, Kim. *The Obsession*. New York: Harper and Row, 1981.

Donovan, Lynn. *The Anti Diet*. New York: Nash Publishers, 1971.

Eichenbaum, Luise and Susie Orbach. *Outside In Inside Out: Women's Psychology: A Feminist Psychoanalytic Approach*. London: Penguin Books, 1982.

Ernst, Sheila and Goodison, Lucy. *In Our Own Words: A Book of Self-Help Therapy*. Boston: Houghton Mifflin, 1981.

MacLeod, Sheila. *The Art of Starvation: Anorexia Observed*. London: Virago, 1981.

Orbach, Susie. *Fat Is A Feminist Issue*. New York: Berkley Books, 1979.

Pearson, Leonard and Lillian. *The Psychologist's Eat Anything Diet*. New York: Wyden Books, 1973.

Rainer, Tristine. *The New Diary: How to Use a Journal for Self-Guidance and Expanded Creativity*. London: Angus and Robertson, 1980.

Schiffman, Muriel. *Gestalt Self Therapy* and *Self Therapy*. Berkeley, Calif.: Self Therapy Press, 1980.

Southgate, John; Randall, Rosemary; and Tomlinson, Frances. *The Barefoot Psychoanalyst: An Illustrated Manual of Self Help Therapy*. London: The Association of Karen Horney Psychoanalytic Counsellors, 1978.

ABOUT THE AUTHOR

Susie Orbach co-founded the Women's Therapy Centre (London, 1976) and the Women's Therapy Centre Institute (New York, 1981). She has worked with hundreds of women on their eating problems. She is currently involved in the post-graduate training of psychotherapists.